Travel English Conversation

Bank

Tourism English Conversation

Ilwoo Park

dongyangbooks

Ilwoo Park

Professor, Hotel Management, Korea Tourism College

Master's Degree in Hospitality Management , Florida International University

Bachelor's Degree in Hospitality Management, Florida International University

Author, *English for Tourism*

Author, *Key Questions and Answers for the Airline Interview*

Travel English Conversation

First published in March 2022

By dongyangbooks

463-16, Dongyang bldg., Seogyo-Dong, Mapo-Gu, Seoul, Korea

Publisher Kim Tae-woong

Editor Hwang Joon

Design Moon-C design

Price 16,500

ISBN 979-11-5768-781-7   13740

www.dongyangbooks.com

Components Main Book / MP3

Introduction

Traveling abroad can be an exciting and lovely experience for everyone! Whether traveling to the great cities in America, visiting the museums and magnificent structures of Europe, or even sightseeing the ancient temples in Asia, a wonderful thing these countries have in common for tourists is that there is only one language everyone needs to know to fully enjoy their vacation overseas. That is English!

Conversely, now imagine you are an employee in the Travel and Service industry. How would you speak to foreigners visiting your country? Travelers from America, Europe, or Asia. What is the common language you would use to communicate with tourists from all the different countries? You guessed it! It's English!

So, this book was written for two types of people in mind: those who want to improve their English speaking abilities to fully enjoy their travel abroad experiences, and for those who are currently (or interested in) working in the tourism industry so they could develop their skills to become greater assets for where they are employed.

The material in each chapter was designed specifically to cater to both travelers and employees in the travel sector. In each chapter the book provides a variety of exercises for students to review and practice the lesson for a better understanding of the material, while offering them the freedom to solve certain problems in a creative and unique way.

- **Need-to-know Vocabulary** provides readers with a list of basic vocabulary words that would be crucial to know in related chapter.

- **Let's Talk** consists of dialogues for students to practice reading and to give exposure of certain situations that might occur.

- **Check Up** tests the students to ensure they have a good understanding of the dialogues from *Let's Talk*.

- **Practice Pattern** offers students a variety of exercises to help them understand grammar and sentence structures.

- **Listen Up** uses MP3 and a variety of exercises for students to enhance their listening skills.

- **Activity** provides students with a variety of unique and different types of exercises for a better comprehension of the material learned throughout the chapter.

- **Build Up** offers students exercises created to encourage students to problem solve in a personal and creative manner.

- **Answer Key** will be provided in the back of the book.

Table of Contents

Travel English Conversation

Unit 01

Reservations before the Flight

Unit 01 Reservations before the Flight

Tourism English Conversation

Need-to-know Vocabulary 1

Fill in the blanks with the correct word and read the finished sentences out loud.

• reserve	• round trip	• depart
• class	• available	• airlines

1   I hope there are flights _____ on January 28th.

2   I will _____ on January 28th and return on February 5th.

3   I will come back, so I need to get _____ tickets.

4   I will not fly economy or business class. I will fly first _____.

5   I need to _____ tickets to go to New York City.

6   I will reserve a ticket with Korean _____.

Let's Talk 1

Practice reading the conversation with a partner and answer the questions under **Check Up 1**.

Airline Staff	Thank you for calling Korean Airlines. How may I help you?
Passenger	I would like to reserve a round trip ticket from Seoul to New York City.
Airline Staff	Sure, when would you like to travel?
Passenger	I want to depart on January 28th and return on February 5th. Do you have a flight available?
Airline Staff	Of course, sir. Would you like an economy, business or first class ticket?
Passenger	I would like to fly first class.
Airline Staff	Wonderful, sir. May I have your name, please?
Passenger	It's James King.

Check Up 1

Circle T for True, or F for False.

1 The passenger wants to leave on January 28th.   **T / F**

2 The passenger is flying business class.   **T / F**

3 The passenger is going to New York City.   **T / F**

Practice Pattern 1

Use the word(s) in the (   ) to answer the question.

1 How may I help you?

I would like + _____ (*reserve*) tickets to go to New York City.

2 When would you like to travel?

I would like + _____ (*depart*) on January 28th.

3 Would you like an economy, business or first class ticket?

I would like + _____ (*fly*) first class.

Listen Up 1

Listen to the sentences and fill in the blanks with the correct word.

1 Thank you for calling Korean _____.

2 I would like to reserve a _____ ticket to New York City.

3 Would you like an _____, business, or first class ticket?

4 I want to _____ on January 28th and _____ on February 5th.

5 Do you have a flight _____?

Activity 1

Practice how to read the dates, months, and days in English and answer the following questions.

- **Dates**

First(1st)	Second(2nd)	Third(3rd)	Fourth(4th)
Fifth(5th)	Sixth(6th)	Seventh(7th)	Eighth(8th)
Ninth(9th)	Tenth(10th)	Eleventh(11th)	Twelfth(12th)
Thirteenth(13th)	Fourteenth(14th)	Fifteenth(15th)	Twentieth(20th)
Twenty-first(21st)	Thirtieth(30th)	Thirty-first(31st)	

- **Days**

Sunday	Monday	Tuesday	Wednesday
Thursday	Friday	Saturday	

- **Months**

January	February	March	April
May	June	July	August
September	October	November	December

1   What date does James King want to leave to New York City?

_____

2   What date does James King want to return to Seoul?

_____

3   What month were you born in?

_____

4   What is your favorite day of the week?

_____

5   What is today's date?

_____

Need-to-know Vocabulary 2

Circle the correct word and read the finished sentences out loud.

> • acceptable   • Visa Card   • aisle   • cancel
> • leave   • passenger   • reservation

1   I need to make a (reservation, acceptable), please.

2   May I have an (aisle, passenger) seat?

3   I would like to pay with a (leave, Visa Card).

4   I would like to (reservation, cancel) my reservation.

5   When will you (leave, aisle)?

6   Is Mastercard (Visa Card, acceptable) for my purchase?

7   I am the only (cancel, passenger).

Let's Talk 2

Practice reading the conversation with a partner and answer the questions under Check Up 2.

 01-03

Airline Staff	Will you be flying alone, Mr. King?
Passenger	Yes, I will be flying alone. I am the only passenger.
Airline Staff	Do you prefer a window seat or an aisle seat?
Passenger	I prefer an aisle seat.
Airline Staff	Okay, Mr. King, I reserved a first class round trip ticket from Seoul to New York City from January 28th until February 5th. Your flight will leave at 10 a.m. and arrive at 11 a.m. Eastern Standard Time. Your total comes to $1,500. How will you be paying?
Passenger	I will be paying with a Visa Card. Is that acceptable?
Airline Staff	Of course, sir. You may pay by Visa Card or Mastercard and can cancel your reservation one week in advance.

> • **pay with a**: I will/I'm going to/I want to ~ [credit card].
> • **pay by**: You can/You may/Can I ~ [credit card]?
> • **pay in**: I will/You can ~ [cash].

Check Up 2

Circle the correct answer choice according to the information in Let's Talk 2.

1 The passenger is flying (with)…

A his wife   **B** his friend   **C** his sister   **D** by himself

2 The passenger wants to sit in the…

A window seat   **B** aisle seat   **C** cockpit   **D** baggage area

3 The passenger can pay for his ticket with…

A Visa Card   **B** cash   **C** Mastercard   **D** check

Practice Pattern 2

Fill in the blanks with the appropriate sentences.

- OK. Your flight will leave at 10 a.m. and how will you be paying?
- Do you prefer a window seat or an aisle seat?
- Will you be flying alone, Mr. King?

1 **Airline Staff** _____

     Passenger I prefer an aisle seat.

2 **Airline Staff** _____

     Passenger I will be paying with a Visa Card.

3 **Airline Staff** _____

     Passenger Yes, I am the only passenger.

Listen Up 2

Listen to the sentences and fill in the blanks with the correct word. 🎧 01-04

1 You may _____ Visa Card or Mastercard.

2 You can cancel your _____ one week in advance.

3 Your flight will _____ at 10 a.m. and _____ at 11 a.m. Eastern Standard Time.

4 Will you be flying _____?

5 Is credit card _____?

Activity 2

Read the conversation in Let's Talk 2 again and circle all of the pictures related to the passenger's information.

credit card

cash

with family

alone

economy class ticket

first class ticket

New York

February 28th

February 5th

window seat

Build Up

Read the conversation below and complete the form.

Airline Staff	Thank you for calling Asiana Airlines. How may I help you?
Passenger	I would like to reserve a round trip ticket from New York City to Tokyo.
Airline Staff	Sure, when would you like to travel?
Passenger	I want to depart on March 3rd and return on May 15th. Do you have a flight available?
Airline Staff	Of course, ma'am. Would you like an economy, business, or first class ticket?
Passenger	I would like to fly economy class.
Airline Staff	Wonderful, ma'am. May I have your name, please?
Passenger	It's Jenny Moon.
Airline Staff	Do you prefer a window seat or an aisle seat?
Passenger	I prefer a window seat.
Airline Staff	Okay, Ms. Moon, I reserved an economy class round trip ticket from New York City to Tokyo from March 3rd until May 15th. Your flight will leave at 10 a.m. and arrive at 3 p.m. Eastern time. Your total comes to $1,800. How will you be paying?
Passenger	I will be paying with a credit card. Is that acceptable?
Airline Staff	Of course, ma'am. You may pay by a Visa Card or Mastercard and can cancel your reservation one week in advance.

Name .... ☐ Mr / ☐ Ms

Date & Time
Depart: .... (AM / PM)   Return: .... (AM / PM)
       MM   DD   TIME   MM   DD   TIME

Destination
From: ....   To: ....

Type
☐ Round Trip   ☐ One-way Trip

Seat
☐ Window Seat   ☐ Aisle Seat

Class
☐ First Class   ☐ Business Class   ☐ Economy Class

Payment
☐ Visa Card   ☐ Cash   ☐ Mastercard

AIRLINES

Unit 02

Airport Check-in

Unit 02 Airport Check-in
Tourism English Conversation

Need-to-know **Vocabulary 1**

Match the words with the correct picture.

- passport
- boarding pass
- scale
- departure time
- boarding gate
- extra charge
- baggage
- baggage claim tag

1

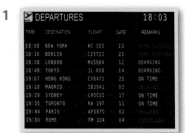

_____

2

_____

3

_____

4

_____

5

_____

6

_____

7

_____

8

_____

Let's Talk 1

Practice reading the conversation with a partner and answer the questions under Check Up 1.

Airline Agent	May I see your passport and boarding pass, please?
Passenger	Here is my passport and E-ticket.
Airline Agent	Thank you. Where are you flying to, today?
Passenger	I will be going to Atlanta, Georgia.
Airline Agent	Do you have any baggage to check-in?
Passenger	I have 2 bags to check-in and 1 carry-on bag.
Airline Agent	Could you put your two bags on the scale? And here are your baggage claim tags. Your luggage is overweight. There will be an extra charge of $75 per bag.
Passenger	That will be fine. Do you accept Visa Card?
Airline Agent	Of course, sir. Everything is complete. Your boarding gate is at F8 and the departure time is at 3 p.m. Be at the boarding gate half an hour prior to departure. Have a wonderful flight.
Passenger	Thank you very much.

These days, people can buy their airplane tickets on the Internet. We call these **E-tickets**. **E = Electronic**. So an **E-ticket** is a ticket bought electronically, such as the Internet. There is no paper copy unlike the tickets you buy at a tour agency. If you want a copy you will have to print it when you receive the **E-ticket** in your E-mail.

Check Up 1

Circle the correct answer or answers.

1   What 2 items does the airline ticketing agent ask to see from the traveler?

A passport   **B** scale   **C** boarding gate   **D** boarding pass

2   How many bags does the passenger want to check-in?

A 1   **B** $75   **C** 2   **D** F8

3   Why does the airline ticketing agent tell the passenger to pay $75?

A The passenger has too many bags.

B The passenger's bags are too heavy.

C The passenger is flying too far away.

D The passenger was late.

Practice Pattern 1

Read the questions and circle the correct response.

1   **Airline Agent**   May I see your passport and boarding pass, please?

   Passenger   **A** Here is my Visa Card.

   B Here is my boarding gate.

   C Here is my passport and boarding pass.

   D Here is my wallet.

2   **Airline Agent**   Do you have any baggage to check-in?

   Passenger   **A** I have 1 bag to carry-on.

   B I have 2 bags to check-in.

   C I have an E-ticket.

   D I have 1 overweight bag.

3   **Airline Agent**   Where are you flying to, today?

   Passenger   **A** I will be going to the boarding gate.

   B I will be going to a wonderful flight.

   C I will be going to Atlanta, Georgia.

   D I will be going to the ticketing agent.

Listen Up 1

Listen to the sentences and fill in the blanks with the correct word.

02-02

1   May I see your _____ and boarding pass?

2   Could you put your luggage on the _____?

3   There will be an _____ of $75.

4   Here are your _____.

5   Your _____ is at 3 p.m.

Activity 1

Fill in the blanks with your own questions and answers to make a new conversation. Practice reading your new conversation with a partner.

Airline Agent   May I see your passport and boarding pass, please?

Passenger   _____

Airline Agent   Where are you flying to, today?

Passenger   _____

Airline Agent   _____

Passenger   I have 1 bag to check-in.

Need-to-know Vocabulary 2

Fill in the blanks with the correct word and read the finished sentences out loud.

• conveyor belt	• belongings	• prohibited
• laptop	• cooperation	• scanner

1 Drugs and knives are _____ items in the airplane. Please throw them away.

2 Thank you for your _____ . We appreciate it very much.

3 If you have a _____ computer, please take it out and put it in the basket.

4 Please step through the _____ when you are ready and raise your arms above your head.

5 Put your bags and laptop on the _____ .

6 Please put your _____ in the basket and put it on the conveyor belt.

Let's Talk 2

Practice reading the conversation with a partner and answer the questions under Check Up 2.

Security Check	Please put all of your belongings on the conveyor belt.
Passenger	What about my laptop?
Security Check	Would you take out your laptop and put it on the conveyor belt?
Passenger	Of course.
Security Check	Please make sure you do not have any prohibited items shown on the chart. If so, you may give them to me.
Passenger	I do not have any prohibited items. Where should I go now?
Security Check	Please step through the scanner when you are ready.
Passenger	Okay.
Security Check	You are all set. Thank you for your cooperation. Have a wonderful flight.
Passenger	Thank you.

> When you are traveling, your **bag** can also be called **baggage**, **luggage**, or **suitcase**.

Check Up 2

Circle T for True, or F for False.

1   The laptop should be placed on the conveyor belt.   **T / F**

2   Prohibited items should be placed on the conveyor belt.   **T / F**

3   The passenger can pass through the scanner when he is ready.   **T / F**

Practice Pattern 2

Answer the passenger's questions using "Would you…" and the word(s) in the (   ).

1   **Passenger**   Where should I put my laptop?

     Security Check   Would you + _____ ? *(conveyor belt)*

2   **Passenger**   Where should I put these items?

     Security Check   Would you + _____ ? *(prohibited items)*

3   **Passenger**   Where should I go now?

     Security Check   Would you + _____ ? *(scanner)*

Listen Up 2

Listen to the sentences and fill in the blanks with the correct word.

1   Where should I put my _____ ?

2   Please put all your belongings on the _____ .

3   Would you step through the _____ when you are ready?

4   Your _____ is much appreciated.

5   You may give me any _____ items you may have.

Activity 2

Listen to the airline announcement and fill in the blanks using the words provided.

• identification	• ten minutes	• boarding	• passengers
• assistance	• announcement	• inviting	• New York City

Good afternoon _____. This is the pre-boarding _____

for Korean Air flight 128 to_____. We are now _____

those passengers with small children and any passengers requiring special

_____, to begin _____ at this time. Please have your

boarding pass and _____ ready. Regular boarding will be in approximately

_____. Thank you.

Build Up

Make a list of items you would take on board and items you would check-in.

For check-in:

    1   wine

    2   perfume

    3   _____

    4   _____

For boarding:

    1   magazine

    2   MP3 player

    3   _____

    4   _____

Unit 03

In the Airplane

Unit 03 In the Airplane
Tourism English Conversation

Need-to-know Vocabulary 1

Use the underlined hints in the sentences to find the correct definition.

• stow	• upright	• overhead bin
• take off	• fasten	• seat belt

1   I need to <u>make this tight</u> so that it will not be loose. _____

2   Stand up <u>straight</u> so I can see how tall you are. _____

3   When will the airplane <u>depart</u>? _____

4   Could you <u>put away</u> your belongings under the seat? _____

5   You should always wear a <u>safety belt</u> to be safe. _____

6   Would you put your luggage in the <u>compartment above your head</u>? _____

Let's Talk 1

Practice reading the conversation with a partner and answer the questions under Check Up 1.

 03-01

Passenger	Excuse me, could you tell me when we will take off?
Flight Attendant	We will be leaving shortly, ma'am.
Passenger	Okay, thank you.
Flight Attendant	Could you stow your baggage in the overhead bin or under the seat in front of you?
Passenger	Could you help me stow away this suitcase? It is too heavy for me to lift.
Flight Attendant	Certainly. Could you also return your seat to the upright position and fasten your seat belt?
Passenger	Could you help me fasten the seat belt? I don't know how to do it.
Flight Attendant	Of course, ma'am.

Flight attendants serve beverages and meals to passengers. They also do their best to make sure everyone has a comfortable flight. Flight attendants may also be called **airline stewardess, airline host, cabin attendant**, and **cabin crew**. A **male flight attendant** can be called an **airline steward** or **airline host**.

Check **Up 1**

Fill in the blanks with the best response.

> **A** The plane will take off shortly.
> **B** To fasten the seat belt.
> **C** The bag is too heavy.

1   What does the Flight Attendant tell the Passenger to do with the seat belt?

   _____

2   Why did the traveler need help with the luggage?

   _____

3   When will the plane take off?

   _____

Practice **Pattern 1**

Look at the flight attendant's responses and fill in the questions using "Could you…" and the word(s) in the (   ).

1   **Passenger**   Could you + _____ ? (*tell me departure time*)

   Flight Attendant   We will take off in just a moment.

2   **Passenger**   Could you + _____ ? (*stow*)

   Flight Attendant   Sure, I will help you right now.

3   **Passenger**   Could you + _____ ? (*fasten seat belt*)

   Flight Attendant   Of course ma'am.

Listen Up 1

Listen to the dialogue and circle the correct answer.

1   When will the plane take off?

   A 10 minutes   **B** 20 minutes   **C** 10 hours   **D** 20 hours

2   Where is the airplane flying to?

   A Paris   **B** London   **C** Rome   **D** Venice

3   What did the traveler need help with?

   A the seat   **B** the luggage   **C** the seat belt   **D** the food

Activity 1

Listen to the airline announcement and fill in the blanks using the words provided.

• fasten	• seat belt	• bin
• luggage	• upright	• stow

Flight Attendant:

Ladies and gentlemen, the Captain has turned on the _____ sign. If you have

not already done so, please _____ your_____ underneath the seat in

front of you or in an overhead _____ . Please take your seat and _____

your seat belt. And also make sure your seats are in their _____ positions.

Thank you very much.

Need-to-know Vocabulary 2

Match the words with the correct picture.

- electronic devices
- beverages
- headset
- call button
- tray table
- monitor

1

2

3

_____

_____

_____

4

5

6

_____

_____

_____

Let's Talk 2

Practice reading the conversation with a partner and answer the questions under Check Up 2.

03-04

Passenger	Excuse me, is it possible to use my laptop right now?
Flight Attendant	Yes, you can use your electronic devices. We will also be serving beverages shortly so you should lower your tray table.
Passenger	Great! How much is it to buy a headset?
Flight Attendant	Headsets are $5.00. Would you like me to bring you one?
Passenger	Yes, here is $5.00.
Flight Attendant	Thank you. If you need anything else, you can press the call button.
Passenger	Thank you.
Flight Attendant	You're welcome.

The following are lists of approved **Electronic Devices** on an airplane.

Mobile Phone/Smart Phone	**Tablet Computers**	**Headphones**
MP3 Player	**Electric Shaver**	**Electronic Games**
Laptop/Notebook Computer	**E-Readers**	**DVD/CD Player**
Bluetooth Devices	**Personal Camera**	**Assistive Medical Devices**

Check Up 2

Circle T for True, or F for False.

1   The flight attendant tells the passenger that using electronic devices are
    allowed.   T / F

2   The passenger should raise the tray table to drink a beverage.   T / F

3   The passengers need 2 headsets.   T / F

Practice Pattern 2

Answer the passenger's question with the best response.

> **A** Yes, would you like me to bring you one?
> **B** Yes, we will be serving beverages shortly.
> **C** Yes, you can use your electronic devices.

1   **Passenger**   Is it possible for me to use my MP3 player?

    Flight Attendant   _____

2   **Passenger**   Is it possible for me to order a can of coke?

    Flight Attendant   _____

3   **Passenger**   Is it possible for me to get a headset?

    Flight Attendant   _____

Listen Up 2

Listen to the sentences and fill in the blanks with the correct word.

1. Could you lower your _____?

2. We will be serving _____ shortly.

3. _____ are $5.00.

4. Is it possible to use _____ right now?

5. If you need anything else, you can press the _____.

Activity 2

Read the passage below and write down all of the items the passenger has requested.

All the passengers boarded the flight and soon after the flight took off, one of the passengers pressed the call button. When a cabin crew member came to the passenger, he asked her, "Could I get a headset, please?" So the cabin crew answered, "Sure, I'll bring you one, sir." After a while, the passenger pressed the call button and the cabin crew member approached him again. "How may I help you, sir?" she asked. The passenger then asked, "Is it possible for me to order a Coke, please?" The cabin crew member replied, "Yes, you may, sir. I'll bring you a Coke right away." After about 10 minutes, the passenger pressed the call button again. The cabin crew member came to him and asked, "Is there anything you need, sir?" The passenger asked the cabin crew member, "Could I get one more blanket?" "Certainly." said the cabin crew member. After another 20 minutes had passed, the passenger pressed the call button again. The cabin crew member came to the passenger and asked, "How may I help you, sir?" The passenger asked, "Could I use my MP3 player?" The cabin crew member answered kindly, "Yes, sir. You may use electronic devices now." While listening to music on his MP3 player, the passenger fell asleep and the cabin crew member passed by with a smile.

• What items does the passenger ask for during the flight?

_____

_____

Build Up

Imagine that you are a flight attendant and you are preparing for takeoff. Read the dialogue below and complete the checklist.

Captain	Did all of the passengers board the airplane?
Flight Attendant	Yes, everyone has boarded the airplane.
Captain	Are all of the overhead bins closed?
Flight Attendant	Yes, all of the overhead bins are closed.
Captain	Have all passengers fastened their seat belts?
Flight Attendant	No, all of the passengers have not fastened their seat belts.
Captain	Are all seats in the upright position?
Flight Attendant	No, the seats are not all in the upright position.
Captain	Are all electronic devices off?
Flight Attendant	Yes, all electronic devices are off.
Captain	Are all the window covers opened?
Flight Attendant	No, the window covers are not all opened.

Checklist Before Taking-off	Yes	No
1 All of the passengers are on board.	☐	☐
2 Overhead bins are closed.	☐	☐
3 Passengers' seat belts are fastened.	☐	☐
4 All seats are in the upright position.	☐	☐
5 Electronic devices are off.	☐	☐
6 All the window covers are opened.	☐	☐

Unit 04

Hotel Check-in

Unit 04 Hotel Check-in
Tourism English Conversation

Need-to-know **Vocabulary 1**

Circle the correct word and read the finished sentences out loud.

- key card
- non-smoking
- bellman
- signature
- registration card
- departure date

1. You will need a (key card, bellmen) to open your door.

2. My (departure date, signature) is on December 8th.

3. The (departure date, bellman) will carry your bags to your room.

4. I do not smoke so I will need a (registration card, non-smoking) room for tonight.

5. Can you fill out this (key card, registration card), please?

6. We will need your (non-smoking, signature) on the bottom of the card.

Let's **Talk 1**

Practice reading the conversation with a partner and answer the questions under **Check Up 1**.

Guest	Hello, I would like to check-in for tonight.
Front Desk Agent	May I have your name, please?
Guest	It is Jeff Bean.
Front Desk Agent	Okay, I see your reservation right here. You reserved a non-smoking, single room, and your departure date is on December 8th. Is this correct?
Guest	Yes, that is my reservation.
Front Desk Agent	Great. Would you just fill out this registration card? I will also need your signature on the bottom of the card.
Guest	Sure. Here you are.
Front Desk Agent	Thank you. Your room number is 601 on the 6th floor. Here is your key card and the bellman will show you to your room.

Guest	Thank you so much.
Front Desk Agent	You're welcome. We hope you enjoy your stay with us.

A **Bellman** is a hotel employee who carries guests' belongings to their room. They are also known by titles such as, **Bellhop**, **Bellboy**, and **Porter**.

Check Up 1

Circle the correct answer.

1   What type of room did the guest reserve?

   A a smoking room   **B** a non-smoking room   **C** a single room   **D** B & C

2   When will the guest be leaving?

   A Room 601   **B** 6th floor   **C** December 8th **D** December 18th

3   Who will show the guest to his room?

   A Jeff Bean   **B** the front desk agent   **C** the bellman   **D** nobody

Practice Pattern 1

Read what the guest has to say and circle the correct response.

1   **Guest**   I would like to check-in for tonight.

   Front Desk Agent   **A** May I have your name?

   B May I have your Visa Card?

   C May I have your signature?

   D May I have your room number?

2   **Guest**   What is my room number?

   Front Desk Agent   **A** Your room number is 6th floor.

   B Your room number is 2016.

   C Your room number is December 8th.

   D Your room number is 601.

3	**Guest**	Where do I need to sign?
	Front Desk Agent	**A** I will need your departure date.
		B I will need your key card.
		C I will need your signature on the bottom of the card.
		D I will need your luggage.

Listen Up 1

Listen to sentences and fill in the blanks with the correct word.

04-02

1   I will need your _____ on the bottom of the _____.

2   My _____ is on December 8th.

3   Here is the _____ to your room.

4   The _____ will show you to your room.

5   I do not smoke, so I requested a _____ room.

Activity 1

For your information, there are various types of rooms in a hotel. Find the right room with the explanation.

• suite room	• twin room	• single room
• family room	• triple room	• double room

1   _____ is a room with a single bed.

2   _____ is a room with a double bed.

3   _____ is a room with 2 separated single beds.

4   _____ is a room with a double bed and one single bed or three separated single beds.

5   _____ is a room with 2 double beds for four people or more, specifically for a family.

6   _____ is a multiple room with more space and furniture including dining and living room, an office, intended for longer staying guests.

Need-to-know Vocabulary 2

Match the words with the correct picture.

- receptionist
- wake-up call
- lobby
- doorman
- concierge

1

_____

2

_____

3

_____

4

_____

5

_____

Let's Talk 2

Practice reading the conversation with a partner and answer the questions under Check Up 2.

Front Desk Agent	Thank you for contacting the receptionist desk. How may I help you?
Guest	I have a really important meeting tomorrow. Can you give me a wake-up call at 7 a.m.?
Front Desk Agent	Of course. Is there anything else we can do for you?
Guest	Who can I speak to if I want to visit a popular restaurant around here?
Front Desk Agent	Our concierge in the lobby will help answer any questions you may have about visiting restaurants and other attractions around town.

Guest	Thank you. By the way, can you call me a taxi for 8 p.m. tonight?
Front Desk Agent	Of course, sir. The doorman will catch one for you when you are ready to leave.
Guest	Thank you!

A **Concierge** is a hotel employee who is in charge of special services for guests. The concierge can make dinner reservations, theater reservations, arrange a tour, etc. In order to become a concierge, you must know a lot about the city and keep up with current trends and entertainment. If you have any questions about restaurants to visit, places to visit, etc., just ask the concierge in your hotel.

Check Up 2

Complete the sentences with the correct answer.

A The receptionist	**B** The concierge	**C** The doorman

1 _____ will give the guest a wake-up call at 7 a.m. tomorrow morning.

2 _____ will help catch a taxi for the guest whenever he is ready to leave.

3 _____ will answer any questions about restaurants and attractions around town.

Practice Pattern 2

Answer the questions about what each hotel employee would do for the guest using "will…" and the word(s) in the (   ).

1 **Question**   What will the receptionist do for the hotel guest?

   Answer   The receptionist will + _____. (*wake-up call*)

2 **Question**   What will the doorman do for the hotel guest?

   Answer   The doorman will + _____. (*taxi*)

3 **Question**   What will the concierge do for the hotel guest?

   Answer   The concierge will + _____. (*dinner reservation*)

Listen Up 2

Listen to the dialogue and circle the correct answer.

1 Who is the hotel guest speaking to?

    A the doorman   **B** the concierge   **C** the receptionist   **D** the restaurant owner

2 What type of food does the concierge recommend to the guest?

    A Indian food   **B** Japanese food   **C** Korean food   **D** Chinese food

3 How do you think the hotel guest will get to the restaurant?

    A by subway   **B** by airplane   **C** by bus   **D** by taxi

Activity 2

Use the directions below to create a new conversation with your partner.

Receptionist	Guest
• Greet the guest • Ask if the guest needs anything • Ask for name, confirm reservation • Ask for any services • Give the key card	• Greet the receptionist • Ask to check-in • Give information to confirm reservation • Ask for a wake-up call at 7 a.m. · Thank the receptionist

Receptionist: (*Greet the guest*) _____

Guest: (*Greet the receptionist*) _____

Receptionist _____

Guest _____

Receptionist _____

Guest _____

Receptionist _____

Guest _____

Receptionist _____

Guest _____

Build Up

Read the dialogue below and check the correct boxes on the registration card.

Guest	Hello, I would like to check-in for tonight.
Front Desk Agent	May I have your name, please?
Guest	It is Jeff Bean.
Front Desk Agent	Okay, I see your reservation right here. You reserved a non-smoking, single room, and your departure date is on December 8th. Is this correct?
Guest	Yes, that is my reservation.
Front Desk Agent	Thank you. Your room number is 601 on the 6th floor. Here is your key card and the bellman will show you to your room.
Guest	Thank you. By the way, I have a really important meeting tomorrow. Can you give me a wake-up call at 7 a.m.?
Front Desk Agent	Of course. Is there anything else we can do for you?
Guest	No, that's all. Thank you.

Reservation	Room Type	Departure Date	Smoking	Special Request
☑ Yes	☐ Single Room	☐ Dec. 4th	☐ Smoking	☐ Wake-up Call
☐ No	☐ Double Room	☐ Dec. 7th	☐ Non-smoking	at _____:_____
	☐ Family Room	☐ Dec. 8th		☐ Breakfast
	☐ Suite	☐ Dec. 21st		☐ Laundry

Conditioner

Body Lotion

Shower Cap

Cotton B

Unit 05

Facilities and Amenities

Facilities and Amenities

Tourism English Conversation

Need-to-know Vocabulary 1

Fill in the blanks with the correct word and read the finished sentences out loud.

> • mini bar   • complimentary   • continental breakfast
> • valuables   • room service   • safe

1   You may find liquor, snacks, and beverages in the _____.

2   The _____ consists of fruits, beverages, muffins, and other pastries.

3   Let's call _____ and eat dinner in our room!

4   What other _____ do you have besides your watch, earrings, necklace, and bracelet?

5   You do not need to pay for breakfast. It is _____.

6   You should keep your watch, jewelry, and other valuables in a _____ so they will not be stolen.

Let's Talk 1

Practice reading the conversation with a partner and answer the questions under Check Up 1.

Front Desk Agent	Hello, how may we help you, ma'am?
Guest	Can you tell me where I can get some breakfast?
Front Desk Agent	Sure, complimentary breakfast is served in the lobby until 10 a.m. Or, you can order meals from our room service if you would like to eat in your room. There is also a mini bar in your room if you wish to just have a snack or a drink.
Guest	There are so many options! What comes out in the breakfast served in the lobby?

Front Desk Agent	Well, it is a Continental breakfast so there will be fruits, beverages, muffins and other pastries.
Guest	That sounds great! By the way, is there somewhere I can put my valuables?
Front Desk Agent	There is a safe next to the mini bar in your room. You can put your valuables in there.
Guest	Thank you for your help.

The 3 types of hotel breakfasts you should know!

Continental is a light meal with fruits, pastries and beverages.

American includes a Continental breakfast but there is also cereal, eggs, meat, pancakes, waffles, or French toast.

English is very similar to the American breakfast, but it comes without pancakes, waffles, or French toast.

Check Up 1

Circle T for True, or F for False.

1 The breakfast served in the lobby is $10.   **T / F**

2 The guest can eat breakfast in the room.   **T / F**

3 Watches, jewelry and other valuables can be stored in a safe.   **T / F**

Practice Pattern 1

Answer the guest's questions using "You can…" and the word(s) in the (   ).

1 **Guest**   How can I order breakfast to my room?

   Front Desk Agent   You can + _____ . (*room service*)

2 **Guest**   Where can I eat breakfast?

   Front Desk Agent   You can + _____ . (*lobby*)

3 **Guest**   Where can I put my valuables?

   Front Desk Agent   You can + _____ . (*safe*)

Listen Up 1

Listen to sentences and fill in the blanks with the correct word.

1 _____ breakfast is served in the lobby.

2 You can order _____ to your room.

3 Fruits, beverages, muffins and other pastries are served in the _____.

4 Where can I put my watch, jewelry, and other _____?

5 You can put your valuables in the _____.

6 The _____ has liquor, snacks, and other beverages.

Activity 1

Where would you find the foods or items in a hotel? Write down the words under the category where you might find them.

• orange juice	• necklace	• earrings	• candy
• whiskey	• Coca-Cola	• chocolate bar	• muffin
• apple	• milk	• watch	• wallet

LOBBY (Breakfast)

MINI BAR

SAFE

Need-to-know Vocabulary 2

Match the words with the correct picture.

- sauna
- swimming pool
- spa
- laundry service
- fitness center
- gift shop

1

_____

2

_____

3

_____

4

_____

5

_____

6

_____

Let's Talk 2

Practice reading the conversation with a partner and answer the questions under Check Up 2.

Guest	Excuse me, where can I go to relax in the hotel?
Front Desk Agent	We have a sauna on the 10th floor if you want to take a steam bath.
Guest	That sounds good! Where can I go to get a massage?
Front Desk Agent	You will want to visit our spa on the 10th floor as well.
Guest	And where can I go to exercise?
Front Desk Agent	You can either visit our fitness center to work out or you can use the swimming pool. They are both on the 15th floor. After you finish

	exercising, you can call the laundry service to get your clothes washed.
Guest	Thank you for your help.
Front Desk Agent	You're very welcome.

Facility vs. Amenity
A **facility** is a place where guests can visit. (swimming pools, saunas, spas, fitness centers)
An **amenity** is a service that is available for the guests. (laundry service, babysitting, Wi-Fi)

Check Up 2

Circle the correct answer.

1   Where can the guest go to take a steam bath?

    A the swimming pool   **B** the fitness center   **C** the sauna   **D** the spa

2   Where can the guest go to swim?

    A the swimming pool   **B** the fitness center   **C** the sauna   **D** the spa

3   Where is the fitness center located?

    A on the 10th floor   **B** on the 15th floor   **C** in the sauna   **D** in the spa

Practice Pattern 2

Fill in the blanks with appropriate sentences.

    A The fitness center is on the 15th floor.
    B The sauna is on the 10th floor.
    C The spa is on the 10th floor.

1   Where is the spa located?

_____

2   Where is the fitness center located?

_____

3   Where is the sauna located?

_____

Listen Up 2

Listen to the sentences and fill in the blanks with the correct word.

1 You should call _____ to get your clothes washed.

2 If you want to swim, you should visit our _____ on the 15th floor.

3 The _____ are on the 10th floor.

4 Is the _____ located on the 4th floor?

5 You can get a relaxing massage at our _____ .

Activity 2

Read the article and fill in the blanks with the correct facilities and amenities for each floor.

8F	⑦ _____
7F	Mr. ⑥ _____ 's room 701
6F	Laundry Service
5F	Mr. King's room 501 Gets a drink from the ⑤ _____
4F	Ms. Dorothy's room 412 Puts her valuables in the ④ _____
3F	Sauna ③ _____
2F	② _____
1F	Concierge Desk Dining Room Today's Menu: ① _____

The Lifetree hotel is one of the most beloved hotels in our city. On the 1st floor, there is a concierge desk and a dining room. Today's breakfast menu is a Continental breakfast. On the 2nd floor is the gift shop. If guests are tired, they may enjoy some time by relaxing in the sauna. They can also work out in the fitness center that is right next to the sauna on the 3rd floor. Ms. Dorothy, one of the guests who is staying on the 4th floor, placed some of her valuables in the safe, while another guest, James King, grabbed a drink from the mini bar in his room. Mr. Arthur who is a long-staying guest, is currently staying in room number 701. Guests can use the laundry service on the 6th floor and may also swim on the top floor of the hotel, while enjoying the sky lounge view.

• swimming pool	• gift shop	• mini bar	• safe
• Continental breakfast	• fitness center	• Arthur	

Build Up

Where would you send the guests?

> Where can I go to swim?
>
> _____

> Where can I eat breakfast?
>
> _____

> Where can I get a snack?
>
> _____

> Where can I put my valuables?
>
> _____

> Where can I buy gifts?
>
> _____

> Where can I take a steam bath?
>
> _____

Unit 06

At a Restaurant

Unit 06 At a Restaurant
Tourism English Conversation

Need-to-know Vocabulary 1

Fill in the blanks with the correct word and read the finished sentences out loud.

> • dessert • vegetarian • appetizer • server
> • menu • specialty • main entrée • recommendation

1   Hello, my name is William and I will be your _____ for tonight.

2   Many people order soup or salad as an _____.

3   I do not eat meat because I am a _____.

4   After the salad, I would like the pasta as my _____.

5   I would like a bowl of ice cream for _____.

6   I need to see the _____ if I want to know what to order.

7   I don't know what is good at this restaurant. Could you give me a _____ on what to eat?

8   Our house _____ is the Surf and Turf. It is a very popular dish.

Let's Talk 1

Practice reading the conversation with a partner and answer the questions under Check Up 1.

Server	Hello, my name is Jeffery and I will be your server for tonight. Do you have any questions about the menu?
Customer	Yes, do you have any recommendations? It is my first time here.
Server	Well, our house specialty is the Surf and Turf. It is a very popular dish. We also have the mixed vegetable meal for vegetarians.
Customer	Great! Can I start with a small salad as an appetizer and the Surf and Turf for my main entrée?

Server	Sure, and what would you like to drink?
Customer	May I have a glass of water, please?
Server	Of course! May I also recommend a bowl of ice cream for dessert?
Customer	That sounds lovely, thank you.

What is a Surf and Turf?

Surf represents the ocean. Therefore, surf refers to a type of seafood.

Turf represents the soil and dirt. Therefore, turf refers to a type of meat.

So, this American cuisine includes both seafood and meat.

Check Up 1

Complete the sentences with the correct answer.

A appetizer	**B** main entrée	**C** dessert

1   The customer will order a bowl of ice cream for _____.

2   The customer will order a Surf and Turf for the _____.

3   The customer will order a small salad as an _____.

Practice Pattern 1

Order food and drinks from the server using "May I..." and the word(s) in the (   ).

1   **Server**   What would you like to drink?

    Customer   May I + _____? (*water*)

2   **Server**   What would you like as an appetizer?

    Customer   May I + _____? (*salad*)

3   **Server**   What would you like as your main entrée?

    Customer   May I + _____? (*Surf and Turf*)

Listen Up 1

Listen to the dialogue and circle the correct answer.

1   What is the name of the server?

    A Stacy   **B** Stella   **C** Stephanie   **D** Susan

2   What kind of soup does the server recommend as an appetizer?

    A chicken noodle   **B** mushroom   **C** broccoli   **D** bean

3   How does the customer want the steak cooked?

    A medium   **B** well done   **C** medium rare   **D** rare

Activity 1

There are many ways to cook a steak. Use the pictures of the different temperatures of the steak and practice ordering with a server.

Customer 1	Customer 2	Customer 3	Customer 4	Customer 5
rare	medium rare	medium	medium well	well done

Server: How would you like your steak?

1   **Customer 1**   I would like my steak, _____.

2   **Customer 2**   I would like my steak, _____.

3   **Customer 3**   I would like my steak, _____.

4   **Customer 4**   I would like my steak, _____.

5   **Customer 5**   I would like my steak, _____.

Need-to-know Vocabulary 2

Use the description below to find the correct vocabulary definition.

• cocktail	• on the rocks	• draft	• liquor
• neat	• bartender	• wine	• beer

1   This person works behind the bar and serves alcoholic beverages to customers.   _____

2   Whiskey, Scotch, Rum, Brandy, and Vodka are popular types of this alcohol.   _____

3   Budweiser, Guinness, and Heineken are popular brands of this alcoholic drink.   _____

4   Ordering a glass of liquor without ice.   _____

5   Ordering a glass of liquor with ice.   _____

6   Mixed drink with a type of liquor and mixture, such as fruit juice or other flavors.   _____

7   Beer served from a cask or barrel.   _____

8   Alcoholic drink made from fermented grapes.   _____

Let's Talk 2

Practice reading the conversation with a partner and answer the questions under Check Up 2.

Bartender	Hello, I'm Elliot and I will be your bartender for tonight. Do you have any questions?
Customer	Yes, what goes inside a "Bloody Mary?"
Bartender	It is a cocktail made with Vodka and tomato juice.
Customer	Can you tell me what beers you have on draft?
Bartender	Sure. We have Budweiser, Guinness, and Heineken on draft.
Customer	Can I just have a glass of Whiskey and a glass of red wine for my wife?
Bartender	Would you like your Whiskey neat or on the rocks?
Customer	I like my Whiskey cold, so I will have it on the rocks, please.

> **White wine** goes well with poultry (chicken, duck, etc.) and fish. White wine is served cold.
> **Red wine** goes well with red meats (beef, lamb, etc.) and pasta. Red wine is served in room temperature (18~23°C or 64~73°F)

Check Up 2

Circle T for True, or F for False.

1	A "Bloody Mary" cocktail is made of Vodka and tomato juice.	**T / F**
2	The customer wants a glass of Whiskey without ice.	**T / F**
3	The customer's wife will have a glass of white wine.	**T / F**

Practice Pattern 2

Read the bartender's questions and circle the correct response.

1   **Bartender**   What would you like to drink?

     Customer   **A** I will have it neat.

                      B It is made with Vodka and tomato juice.

                      C I will have a glass of red wine.

                      D I like my Whiskey cold.

2   **Customer**   Can you tell me which beers you have on draft?

     Bartender   **A** May I have a Heineken?

                      B We have Budweiser, Guinness, and Heineken.

                      C I will have the "Bloody Mary."

                      D It is made with Vodka and tomato juice.

3   **Bartender**   Would you like the Whiskey with or without ice?

     Customer   **A** Can I have it on the rocks, please?

                      B May I have a glass of red wine?

                      C I will have a Heineken.

                      D What beers do you have on draft?

Listen Up 2

Listen to sentences and fill in the blanks with the correct word.

1   Hello, I am Joe and I will be your _____ for tonight.

2   My favorite _____ are Whiskey and Scotch.

3   May I have a glass of red _____ with my steak?

4   A "Bloody Mary" is a refreshing _____ on a hot day.

5   I don't like it cold so I will take the Whiskey _____.

Activity 2

What are the types of beers, wine and liquor? Write the words under the right category.

- Budweiser
- Whiskey
- Scotch
- Guinness
- Merlot
- Chardonnay
- Heineken
- Rum

BEER

WINE

LIQUOR

Build Up

Read the dialogue and check the order forms below.

Server	Hello, my name is Laura and I will be your server for tonight.
Customer	OK. Do you have any recommendations? It's my first time here.
Server	Well, our house specialty is the Surf and Turf. And we also have a salad menu for vegetarians.
Customer	Great! Can I start with a small salad as an appetizer and the steak for my main entrée?
Server	Sure. How would you like your steak, sir?
Customer	I would like it medium rare, please.
Server	Very well, sir. And what would you like to drink?
Customer	I would like a cocktail. What goes inside a "Bloody Mary?"
Server	It is a cocktail made with Vodka and tomato juice.
Customer	Oh, then I would like a beer. Can you tell me which beers you have on draft?
Server	Sure. We have Budweiser, Guinness, and Heineken on draft.
Customer	Okay, I will have a glass of Heineken.
Server	Yes, sir. Could I recommend you a bowl of ice cream for dessert?
Customer	OK, that would be nice.
Server	Thank you, sir. I will be right away with your salad, first.

Restaurant Order Form

Appetizer	Main Entree	Steak	Drink	Dessert
☐ Soup	☐ Pasta	☐ Rare	☐ Cocktail	☐ Muffin
☐ Salad	☐ Pizza	☐ Medium rare	☐ Heineken	☐ Cheesecake
☐ Muesli	☐ Steak	☐ Medium	☐ Budweiser	☐ Ice cream
		☐ Medium well	☐ Cognac	☐ Coffee
		☐ Well done	☐ Guinness	☐ Pudding

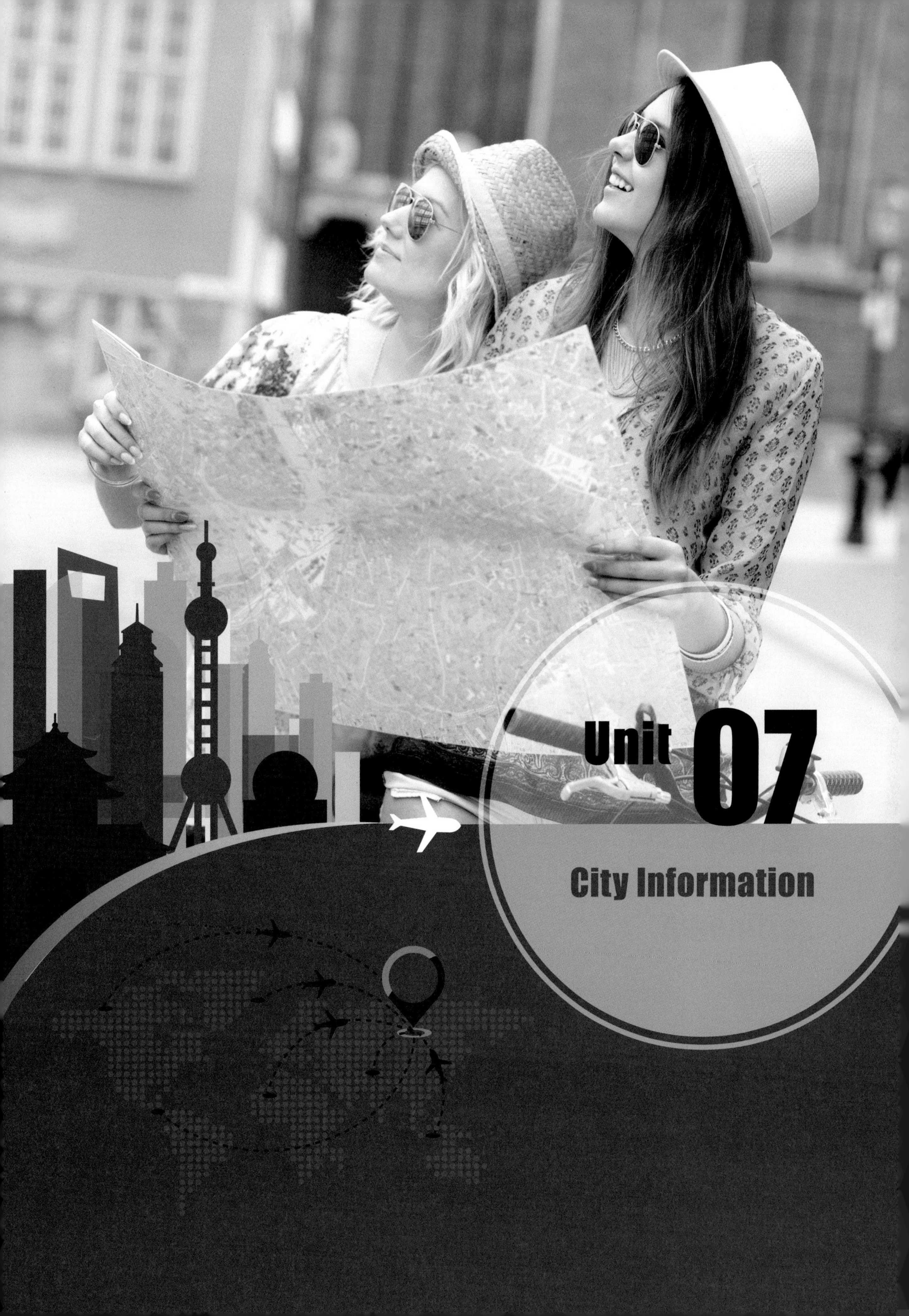

Unit 07

City Information

Unit 07 City Information
Tourism English Conversation

Need-to-know Vocabulary 1

Fill in the blanks with the correct word and read the finished sentences out loud.

• museum	• tour guide	• entrance fee	• sunny
• photographs	• theater	• overcast	• attractions

1   The sky is _____. There are so many clouds today!

2   Hello, my name is Anna and I will be your _____ today. I will show you around the city.

3   You must pay an _____ of $10.00 if you want to go inside.

4   We can learn about the city's history and see beautiful artwork at the _____.

5   I will take many _____ of the city with my new camera.

6   The weather is _____. We will not need an umbrella.

7   You should visit the _____ to watch popular films and musicals.

8   I am so excited to see all the popular _____ in the city.

Let's Talk 1

Practice reading the conversation with a partner and answer the questions under Check Up 1.

Tour Guide	Hello, everyone! My name is Anna and I will be your tour guide today.
Tourist	Hi, Anna! Where will you be taking us today?
Tour Guide	I will take you to all the popular attractions in this city. You will be able to visit the Art Museum and the Palmetto Theater today.
Tourist	How much is the entrance fee for the museum?
Tour Guide	It is $10.00 for adults and $5.00 for children. Once you go inside, you will be able to take many photographs.

Tourist	It is a good idea to be inside, because the day is overcast. Should we take an umbrella?
Tour Guide	You will not need an umbrella. It will be sunny soon.
Tourist	Okay, thanks!

In some attractions, there might not be an entrance fee. That means people can get in without paying any money. The following words and phrases can be used to express this.

FREE   FREE OF CHARGE   FREE OF COST   NO ENTRANCE FEE   NO FEE   NO CHARGE

Check Up 1

Circle the correct answer.

1   What can the tourists do once they are inside the museum?

   A take photographs   **B** pay the entrance fee

   C watch a film   **D** take an umbrella

2   How much is the entrance fee for children?

   A $10.00   **B** $10.50   **C** $5.00   **D** $15.00

3   Why does the tourist say it is a good idea to be inside?

   A It is sunny.   **B** It is raining.   **C** It is overcast.   **D** It is snowing.

Practice Pattern 1

Answer the tourist's questions using "be able to…" and the word(s) in the (   ).

1   **Tourist**   Where will we visit today?

   Tour Guide   You will be able to + _____ . (*museum and theater*)

2   **Tourist**   Can we take photographs inside the museum?

   Tour Guide   You will be able to + _____ . (*photographs*)

3   **Tourist**   What can we see at the theater?

   Tour Guide   You will be able to + _____ . (*film*)

Listen Up 1

Listen to the dialogue and circle the correct answer.

1   What is the name of the theater the tourists will visit?

   A Hello Theater   **B** Dawn Theater   **C** Palm Theater   **D** Palmetto Theater

2   When will the group eat lunch?

   A after the museum   **B** after the theater   **C** before the tour   **D** now

3   What will the group most likely eat for lunch?

   A steak   **B** noodles   **C** hamburgers   **D** pizza

Activity 1

Look at the itinerary and answer the questions with a partner.

TODAY's TOUR SCHEDULE!
(Friday, March 25th, 2022)

TIME	TO DO	
09:00 a.m.	Depart the hotel	
09:30 a.m.	Arrive at Art Museum:	Explore Museum
		Take photographs
11:30 a.m.	Depart Art Museum	
12:00 p.m.	Arrive at Noah's Pizza:	Lunch
01:00 p.m.	Depart Noah's Pizza	
01:30 p.m.	Arrive at South Beach:	Visit Shopping Center
		Beach Volleyball
		Explore on your own
03:00 p.m.	Depart South Beach	
03:30 p.m.	Arrive at Palmetto Theater:	Watch Film, "38 Downtown"
		Take photographs
06:00 p.m.	Depart Palmetto Theater	
06:30 p.m.	Arrive at Annaeli Café:	Dinner
08:30 p.m.	Depart Annaeli Café	
09:00 p.m.	Arrive at the hotel	

1   Where will the tourist go at 9:00 a.m.?

   _____

2   What 3 things can the tourists do at 1:30 p.m.?

   _____

3   Where will the tourists eat lunch?

   _____

4   What is the name of the film tourists can watch at the theater?

   _____

5   What time will the tourists return to the hotel?

   _____

Need-to-know Vocabulary 2

Match the words with the correct picture.

- traffic light
- crosswalk
- sidewalk
- intersection
- pedestrian
- bike route

1

_____

2

_____

3

_____

4

_____

5

_____

6

_____

Let's Talk 2

Practice reading the conversation with a partner and answer the questions under Check Up 2.

Tourist	Excuse me, can you tell me how to get to the hotel?
Tour Guide	Sure, remember to take the sidewalk for pedestrians to be safe.
Tourist	Of course! I don't want to get into an accident.
Tour Guide	Okay, start at the traffic light and go straight until you reach the intersection.
Tourist	Go straight until the intersection?
Tour Guide	That's right. At the intersection, you need to turn left and you will see the hotel on the left side.

Tourist	Thank you for your help!
Tour Guide	You're welcome!

If you go in a clockwise direction, you will see N, E, S, W, on the compass. An easy way to remember the directions is by remembering the following acronyms:

Never	**Eat**	**Soggy**	**Waffles**
North	**East**	**South**	**West**

Check Up 2

Circle T for True, or F for False.

1 The tourist wants the directions to the hotel. **T / F**

2 The tourist should not use the sidewalk to be safe. **T / F**

3 The tourist will see the hotel on the right side. **T / F**

Practice Pattern 2

Put the following sentences in the correct order to make a complete dialogue between the tourist and the tour guide.

A You're welcome.

B Sure, start at the traffic light and go straight until you reach the intersection.

C Yes, at the intersection, you will need to turn left and you will see the hotel on the left side.

D OK. Thank you for your help.

E Excuse me, can you tell me how to get to the hotel?

F I keep going until I reach the intersection?

Tourist _____

Tour Guide _____

Tourist _____

Tour Guide _____

Tourist _____

Tour Guide _____

Listen Up 2

Listen to the conversation and fill in the blanks.

Tourist   Excuse me, can you tell me how to get to the _____ ?

Tour Guide   Sure, start at the _____ and go straight until you reach the

                _____ . At the intersection you will need to turn _____ and

                you will see the hotel on the _____ side.

Tourist   Thank you for your help.

Activity 2

Using the phrases below, practice giving directions with your partner using the map.

• Go straight	• Continue	• Turn left/right	• Make a left/right

- **A** Hospital
- **B** Circus
- **C** Gas Station
- **D** Factory

1   How can the tourist get to B from A?

_____

2   How can the tourist get to C from A?

_____

3   How can the tourist get to D from A?

_____

Build Up

Imagine you are a tour guide leading a group today! Explain to the group how much the entrance fee will be on their next stop.

Situation

Your tour group is about to enter the National Museum. How much is the entrance fee for your group? (Tour guides may enter for free)

Tourists   **6 people**

Tom 63 years old	**Wendy** 32 years old	**Merry** 18 years old
John 28 years old	**Timmy** 5 years old	**Gwen** 45 years old

National Museum Entrance Fee

Kids under 6	Students under 18	Adults	Seniors (over 60)
$5.00 (Free on weekends)	$10.00 (Half off on weekends)	$20.00	Free of cost

1   The entrance fee for your group will be $_____ if you go on Friday.

2   The entrance fee for your group will be $_____ if you go on Saturday.

Unit **08**

Transportation

Unit 08 Transportation
Tourism English Conversation

Need-to-know **Vocabulary 1**

Fill in the blanks with the correct word and read the finished sentences out loud.

> • subway station　　　• bus stop　　　　　• taxi stand
> • destination　　　　　• heavy traffic

1　Go underground to the _____ if you want to take the subway.

2　I need your help. Could you tell me the directions for me to get to my _____?

3　The cars in front of us are not moving because of the _____ at this hour.

4　If you need to take the bus, you should go to the _____.

5　If you are in a hurry, catch a taxi at the _____.

Let's **Talk 1**

Practice reading the conversation with a partner and answer the questions under Check Up 1.　🎧 08-01

Tourist	Excuse me, I was wondering if you could tell me what to take to get to the park?
Tour Guide	Sure, you could go to the subway station and take the subway.
Tourist	What if I take the bus at the bus stop or a taxi at the taxi stand?
Tour Guide	I do not recommend taking the bus or taxi.
Tourist	Why do you say that?
Tour Guide	At this time, there will be heavy traffic on the streets.
Tourist	Thank you, I will take the subway to my destination.
Tour Guide	You're welcome.

Some vocabulary words you hear might have different meanings in the United Kingdom and America. Look at the list below and see how the vocabulary differs depending on where you are.

USA	VS.	UK		USA	VS.	UK
Schedule		Timetable		Subway		Underground (or Tube)
Sidewalk		Pavement		Taxi stand		Taxi rank
Bus		Coach		Truck		Lorry

Check Up 1

Complete the sentences with the correct answer.

A heavy traffic	**B** subway	**C** park

1   The tourist wants to get to the _____ .

2   The tour guide tells the tourist to take the _____ .

3   The tour guide does not recommend taking the bus or taxi because of _____ .

Practice Pattern 1

Look at the tour guide's responses and fill in the questions using "I was wondering if…" and the word(s) in the (   ).

1   **Tourist**   I was wondering if + _____ . (*get to the park*)

     Tour Guide   Sure! You could go to the subway station and take the subway.

2   **Tourist**   I was wondering if + _____ . (*take the bus*)

     Tour Guide   I would not recommend taking the bus.

3   **Tourist**   I was wondering if + _____ . (*take a taxi*)

     Tour Guide   I would not recommend taking a taxi.

Listen Up 1

Listen to sentences and fill in the blanks with the correct word.

08-02

1   You could go to the _____ and take the subway.

2   If you are in a hurry, you should take a taxi at the _____.

3   At this time, there will be _____ on the streets.

4   How can I get to my _____ from here?

5   Let's wait at the _____ and take the bus to the park!

Activity 1

Fill in the missing letters for the vocabulary words. Then form a new sentence for each word.

1   s __ bw __ y   _____

2   t __ x __ st __ n __   _____

3   __ es __ in __ tio __   _____

4   h __ av __ t __ af __ ic   _____

5   b __ s s __ op   _____

6   d __ re __ t __ ons   _____

Need-to-know Vocabulary 2

Circle the correct word and read the finished sentences out loud.

> • transfer   • fare   • platform
>
> • ticket machine   • express

1   If you are in a hurry, you should ride the (fare, express) train.

2   Go to (platform, transfer) number 3 to get on the subway.

3   You can buy a ticket at the (ticket machine, express) over there.

4   The (platform, fare) for the subway is $1.00.

5   To get to your destination, you must (transfer, ticket machine) at this stop.

Let's Talk 2

Practice reading the conversation with a partner and answer the questions under **Check Up 2**.

 08-03

Tourist	Do you think I should take the subway to get to the park?
Tour Guide	Yes. The subway will be faster because of the heavy traffic on the streets.
Tourist	Can you tell me how to get to the park by subway?
Tour Guide	Of course. First, you have to buy a ticket at the ticket machine and get on the subway car at platform number 3.
Tourist	How much is the subway fare?
Tour Guide	The fare is $1.00 per person and the express fare is $2.00 per person. The express train has fewer stops and will take you to your destination quicker.
Tourist	Do I need to transfer?
Tour Guide	No, just stay on the train until you reach Central Park Station.

$1.00 **per person** means it is $1.00 for every individual. This idiom means, "For a person or for an individual." Other idioms you can use are: **A person**   **A head**   **Per head**

Check Up 2

Circle the correct answer.

1 Where can the tourist buy a ticket for the subway?

    A heavy traffic   **B** platform 3   **C** ticket machine   **D** park

2 Where should the tourist get on the subway?

    A platform 1   **B** platform 2   **C** platform 3   **D** platform 4

3 How much is the fare for an express train?

    A $1.00   **B** $2.00   **C** $3.00   **D** free of charge

Practice Pattern 2

Unscramble the words in the questions the tourist is asking. Use the tour guide's response as a hint.

1 **Tourist**   _____? (tell / how / get / Can / me/ you / to / there)

    Tour Guide   Of course. First, you have to buy a ticket at the ticket machine.

2 **Tourist**   _____? (subway / much / is / the / How / fare)

    Tour Guide   The fare is $1.00 per person.

3 **Tourist**   _____? (transfer / I / to / all / at / Do / need)

    Tour Guide   No, just stay on the train until you reach Central Park Station.

Listen Up 2

Listen to the sentences and fill in the blanks with the correct word.

1 The _____ has fewer stops so you will get there faster.

2 You do not need to _____. Just stay on the train until you arrive.

3 You have to buy a ticket at the _____.

4 You must get on the subway at _____ number 3.

5 The _____ is $1.00 per person and $2.00 per person for the express train.

Activity 2

Look at the Seoul Subway Map and practice giving directions using the following phrases.

- Take the (Color or Number) line.
- Get off at (Name of station) Station.
- Transfer to the (Color or Number) line.

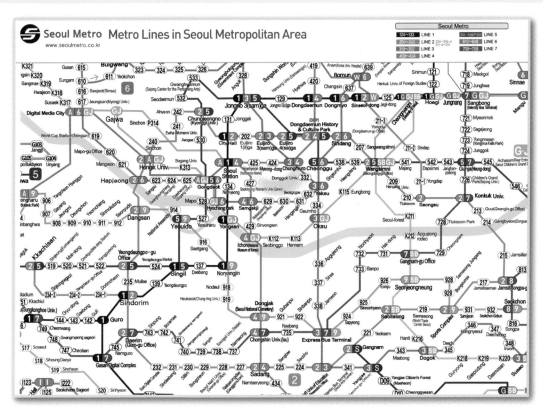

1   **Tourist**   Excuse me, how can I get to the Shopping District in Myeongdong Station from Gangnam Station?

    You   You can take the <u>green line</u> to <u>Sadang</u> Station. Transfer to the line number <u>4</u> and get off at Myeongdong Station.

2   **Tourist**   Excuse me, how can I get to Time Square Department Store in Yeongdeungpo Station from Shinchon Station?

    You   At Shinchon Station you can take the _____ line to _____ Station. Get off there and transfer to the _____ line heading for Seoul Station and get off at Yeongdeungpo Station.

3   **Tourist**   Excuse me, how can I get to City Hall Station from Yeouido Station?

    You   Take this line towards Chungjeongno Station and get off _____ . Transfer to the _____ line towards Euljiro 3ga. City Hall Station is only one stop away.

Build Up

Imagine that you are a veteran tour guide in London, England. Explain the transit directions and the estimated time it will take using the hints in the box. (All directions are fictional.)

From	To
West Minster Abbey	Buckingham Palace

→

1 By Subway (Time: 30 minutes)

1. Go along Abbey Street.
2. Turn left at the corner.
3. There is a subway station after the turn.
4. Line 3 to Palace Station.
5. Go 7 stops.
6. Destination on Queen's Street.

Your explanation:

_____

_____

_____

_____

_____

2 By Bus (Time: 40 minutes)

1. Go straight until you see the crosswalk.
2. Bus stop next to the crosswalk.
3. Bus number 1 heading for Queen's Street.
4. Get off at Palace Station.
5. Destination on the right of the station.

Your explanation:

_____

_____

_____

_____

_____

Unit **09**

Shopping

Unit 09 Shopping

Tourism English Conversation

Need-to-know Vocabulary 1

Fill in the blanks with the correct word and read the finished sentences out loud.

> • souvenir　　　　　• exchange rate　　　　　• sale
> • duty free　　　　　• currency　　　　　• price

1　Can you tell me the _____ for the US dollar to the Korean won?

2　The _____ for this shirt is $20.00

3　You can buy tax-free items at the _____ store.

4　We accept almost all _____ from the dollar, euro, won, and the yen.

5　Where can I buy a _____ for my family and friends back home?

6　If you want to save money, look for items that are on _____ .

Let's Talk 1

Practice reading the conversation with a partner and answer the questions under **Check Up 1**.

09-01

Tourist	Excuse me, do you accept Korean won at this duty free store?
Salesperson	Of course, ma'am. We accept almost all currency from dollar, euro, won, and yen.
Tourist	Can you tell me the exchange rate for the dollar to won?
Salesperson	Sure, 1 US dollar is 1,036 won.
Tourist	Thank you! Can you also recommend a souvenir I can get for my family and friends?
Salesperson	How about this box of chocolates? It is a very popular gift. The price was $20.00, but it is now on sale for $10.00.
Tourist	That sounds great! I will buy it.
Salesperson	Okay!

Here are some similar words for "**Price**." You may hear when you are out shopping or on a tour.

| Rate | Fee | Cost | Fare | Amount | Expense |

Check **Up 1**

Circle T for True, or F for False.

1   The duty free store only accepts US dollars and Korean won.   **T / F**

2   The box of chocolates is a very popular souvenir.   **T / F**

3   The tourist will pay $20.00 for the souvenir.   **T / F**

Practice **Pattern 1**

Look at the salesperson's response and fill in the questions using "How much is…" and the word(s) in the (   ).

1   **Tourist**   How much is + _____? (*box of chocolates*)

    Salesperson   The price for this box of chocolates is $20.00.

2   **Tourist**   How much is + _____? (*T-shirt*)

    Salesperson   The price for this T-shirt is $15.00.

3   **Tourist**   How much is + _____? (*perfume*)

    Salesperson   The price for this perfume is $50.00.

Listen **Up 1**

Listen to the conversation and fill in the blanks with the correct word.   🎧 09-02

1   I would like to recommend this item for you to buy as a _____ for your family and friends.

2   The _____ for this shirt was $20.00 but it is now on _____ for $15.00.

3   You can buy many _____ at the _____ store.

4   We accept all forms of _____ at our store.

5   Can you tell me the _____ for the dollar to won?

Activity 1

Look at the pictures of the US currency and answer how many bills and coins you would use to make up the amount shown.

Cents

Penny	Nickel	Dime	Quarter
$0.01	$0.05	$0.10	$0.25

Dollars

1 Dollar	5 Dollar	10 Dollar	20 Dollar	50 Dollar	100 Dollar
$1.00	$5.00	$10.00	$20.00	$50.00	$100.00

How many of the bills and coins would you use to pay the following prices?

<u>Example</u>

1. $5.50

A. <u>1</u> $5.00 bill

B. <u>2</u> Quarters

2. $6.76

A. <u>1</u> $5.00 bill

B. <u>1</u> $1.00 bill

C. <u>3</u> Quarters

D. <u>1</u> Penny

3. $15.55

A. <u>1</u> $10.00 bill

B. <u>1</u> $5.00 bill

C. <u>2</u> Quarters

D. <u>1</u> Nickel

4. $24.31

A. _____ $20.00 bill

B. _____ $1.00 bills

C. _____ Quarter

D. _____ Nickel

E. _____ Penny

5. $54.06

A. _____ $50.00 bill

B. _____ $1.00 bills

C. _____ Nickel

D. _____ Penny

6. $103.23

A. _____ $100 bill

B. _____ $1.00 bill

C. _____ Dimes

D. _____ Pennies

Need-to-know Vocabulary 2

Fill in the blanks with the correct word and read the finished sentences out loud.

• fitting room	• refund	• receipt
• exchange	• expensive	• cheap

1   Can I _____ this shirt for a bigger size? This one is too small.

2   You may use the _____ to try on the clothes. Tell me if you need a bigger size.

3   If you want your money back, return the item and ask for a _____.

4   This item is on sale so the price is very _____.

5   If you want to remember how much you paid for the shirt, just look at the _____.

6   The price for this shirt is too _____. I don't think I have enough money to buy it.

Let's Talk 2

Practice reading the conversation with a partner and answer the questions under Check Up 2.

Tourist	Excuse me, this shirt is too expensive for me. Do you have something less expensive?
Salesperson	If you look at the shirts that are on sale, you will find a shirt for a cheap price. The fitting rooms are over there if you would like to try on the clothes.
Tourist	I will not need to use the fitting room. I am ready to buy this shirt now.
Salesperson	Great! The total price for the shirt is $10.00. You should keep the receipt if you want to exchange shirts or return it for a refund.
Tourist	Thank you, I will not lose the receipt.
Salesperson	You're welcome. Have a wonderful day!

Try on = To wear the clothes in a fitting room to check the size and how it fits

Check Up 2

Circle the correct answer.

1   What did the tourist buy at the store?

    A a receipt   **B** a fitting room   **C** a cheap shirt   **D** a refund

2   What did the tourist not need to use?

    A a receipt   **B** a fitting room   **C** a cheap shirt   **D** a refund

3   What should the tourist keep if he wants a refund?

    A the receipt   **B** a fitting room   **C** a cheap shirt   **D** a refund

Practice Pattern 2

Put the following sentences in correct order to make a complete dialogue between the tourist and the salesperson.

A I will not need to use the fitting room. I would like to buy this shirt now.

B Thank you, I will not lose the receipt.

C Excuse me, do you have a shirt that is less expensive?

D Sure, the total price is $10.00. You should keep the receipt if you want to exchange shirts or return it for a refund.

E You're welcome. Have a nice day!

F If you look at the shirts that are on sale, you will find a shirt for a cheap price. The fitting rooms are over there if you would like to try on the clothes.

Tourist _____

Salesperson _____

Tourist _____

Salesperson _____

Tourist _____

Salesperson _____

Listen Up 2

Listen to the conversation and fill in the blanks.

Tourist	Excuse me, do you have a shirt less _____?
Salesperson	If you look at the shirts that are on sale, you will find a shirt for a _____ price. The _____ are over there if you would like to try on the clothes.
Tourist	No, thank you. I will not need to use the fitting room. I would like to buy this shirt now.
Salesperson	Sure! The price is $10.00. You should keep the _____ if you want to _____ shirts or return it for a _____ .

Activity 2

Use the directions in the box to make a new conversation.

Situation

Salesperson	Tourist
• Tell the tourist all of the currency you accept. • Tell the tourist that 1 Euro = 1,400 Won. • Tell the tourist that the T-shirt is 30 Euros. • Tell the tourist that you do accept Mastercard.	• Ask the salesperson what currency the store accepts. • Ask the salesperson the exchange rate for Euro to Won • Ask the salesperson how much a T-shirt costs. • Ask if they accept Mastercard.

Tourist	_____
Salesperson	_____
Tourist	_____
Salesperson	_____
Tourist	_____
Salesperson	_____
Tourist	_____
Salesperson	_____

Build Up

Tell the tourists how much they have to pay for the souvenirs.

Souvenir shop

$2.00	$5.00	$5.00	$3.00	$10.00
$20.00	$0.50	$1.50	$20.00	$15.00

1 **Tourist** I want to buy a pen, 2 boxes of chocolates and a T-shirt. How much do I have to pay?

You The total is _____ dollars.

2 **Tourist** I'll buy 2 magnets, 1 bag and a watch for my father. How much are they?

You The total is _____ dollars.

3 **Tourist** I would like to buy a doll for my daughter, 2 postcards and a notepad as souvenirs. I'm going to pay in cash. How much do they cost?

You The total is _____ dollars.

Unit 10

Complaints

Unit 10 Complaints

Tourism English Conversation

Need-to-know Vocabulary 1

Use the underlined hints in the sentences to find the correct definition.

• inconvenience	• odor	• noisy	• mess
• maintenance	• defective	• assure	• apologize

1   There is a really bad <u>smell</u> coming from the sink.   _____

2   We <u>are sorry</u> about this. We will fix it right away.   _____

3   We are sorry for the <u>trouble</u> you are in. We will do our best to help you.   _____

4   I am so sorry about this. I <u>promise</u> that It will not happen again.   _____

5   We will send a <u>repairman</u> to your room right away to fix it.   _____

6   The TV remote control seems <u>to be broken</u>. Can you fix it for me?   _____

7   This room is so <u>dirty</u>. We should call housekeeping right away!   _____

8   The people in the next room are too <u>loud</u>. I cannot sleep.   _____

Let's Talk 1

Practice reading the conversation with a partner and answer the questions under **Check Up 1**.

Guest	Excuse me, I'm afraid I have a few complaints about my room.
Front Desk Agent	What seems to be the problem, sir?
Guest	My room is a mess and has a bad odor coming from the sink. Is it possible to send someone up to fix this?
Front Desk Agent	We apologize about the inconvenience. We will send maintenance to your room right away to fix the sink and housekeeping to clean the room.

Guest	Also, the TV remote control seems defective and the people in the next room are too noisy. I cannot sleep.
Front Desk Agent	We apologize again. We will fix this right away.
Guest	Thank you.
Front Desk Agent	We assure you that this will not happen again.

"**I'm afraid**" usually means I'm scared. But did you know, it also means "**I'm sorry?**" I'm afraid = I'm sorry

Check Up 1
Circle T for True, or F for False.

1   The guest only had one problem with his room.   **T / F**

2   Maintenance will go to the room to clean the room.   **T / F**

3   The people in the next room are being too loud.   **T / F**

Practice Pattern 1
Look at the Front Desk Agent's response and fill in the questions using "Is it possible to…" and the word(s) in the (   ).

1   **Guest**   Is it possible to + _____? (*room*)
    Front Desk Agent   We will send housekeeping to your room right away to clean the room.

2   **Guest**   Is it possible to + _____? (*odor*)
    Front Desk Agent   We will send maintenance to your room right away to fix the sink.

3   **Guest**   Is it possible to + _____? (*TV remote control*)
    Front Desk Agent   We will send maintenance to your room right away to fix the TV remote control.

Listen Up 1

Listen to the sentences and fill in the blanks with the correct word.

1   My room is a _____ and there is a bad _____ coming from the sink.

2   We will send _____ to your room right away to fix the sink.

3   The people in the next door are too _____. I cannot sleep.

4   The TV remote control seems _____. Can you fix it?

5   We _____ you that this will not happen again.

Activity 1

Unscramble the underlined words.

1   There is a bad <u>door</u> coming from the sink.   _____

2   We are so sorry about the <u>oncecennnivei</u>.   _____

3   My TV remote control seems <u>eetidefvc</u>.   _____

4   The people in the next room are too <u>sonyi</u>.   _____

5   My room is such a <u>smes</u>!   _____

6   We <u>usrase</u> you that this will not happen again   _____

7   We will send <u>naaiteecnnm</u> to your room right away to fix the sink.   _____

8   We <u>ozgaiploe</u> again for the inconvenience.   _____

Need-to-know Vocabulary 2

Fill in the blanks with the correct word and read the finished sentences out loud.

• deduct	• gift certificate	• replace
• unsatisfied	• on the house	• mistake

1   You may use this _____ for $20.00 on your next visit to our restaurant.

2   We were _____ with the service. Our server was rude and slow to bring our meal.

3   I apologize for bringing the wrong wine. Let me _____ this glass of wine with a new one.

4   May we offer you a dessert _____?

5   That was my _____. I was very confused and brought out the wrong meal.

6   I did not order this. Please _____ this from my bill.

Let's Talk 2

Practice reading the conversation with a partner and answer the questions under Check Up 2.

Customer	Excuse me, I was very unsatisfied with the service today.
Manager	What seems to be the problem, sir?
Customer	The server made a mistake with my meal but he did not replace it or deduct it from the bill.
Manager	I apologize for the inconvenience. May I offer you a dessert on the house?
Customer	Sure, that will be fine.
Manager	I would also like to give you this gift certificate for $20.00. You may use this gift certificate on your next visit to our restaurant.
Customer	Thank you very much. I feel much better now.
Manager	You're welcome and I assure you that this will not happen again.

Check Up 2

Circle the correct answer.

1   What should the server have replaced to fix the mistake?

    A the bill   **B** the meal   **C** the house   **D** the dessert

2   What did the manager give to the customer "on the house?"

    A a house   **B** a bill   **C** a dessert   **D** inconvenience

3   When can the guest use the gift certificate?

    A today   **B** on the next visit   **C** never   **D** $20.00

Practice Pattern 2

Unscramble the Manager's questions or the Customer's answers and rewrite them in the provided space.

1   **Manager**   What seems to be the problem, sir?

    Customer   (server / mistake / The / made / with / a / meal / my)

    _____.

2   **Manager**   (dessert / the / I / you / house / offer / a / May / on)

    _____?

    Customer   Sure, that will be fine.

3   **Customer**   Thank you very much, I feel much better now.

    Manager   (assure / that / I / will / happen / this / again / not / you)

    _____.

Listen Up 2

Listen to the dialogue and circle the correct answer.

1   What did the server bring the customer by mistake?

    A a dessert   **B** an apology   **C** a soup   **D** a salad

2   What type of menu did the customer ask for?

    A beverage menu   **B** appetizer menu   **C** entrée menu   **D** dessert menu

3   What did the customer order for dessert?

    A cherry pie   **B** apple pie   **C** strawberry pie   **D** blueberry pie

Activity 2

Study the 3A's in handling complaints and practice dealing with customer's complaints.

As an employee in tourism industry, it is important to know how to deal with complaints, especially when there was a mistake. An easy way to do this is to remember the 3A's.

A1 Apology	First, apologize and say you are sorry to the customer.
A2 Action	Second, take action and do something to make the customer feel better.
A3 Assurance	Third, apologize again and assure the customer that it will not happen again.

Number 1 has been done for you. Look at the sample and do numbers 2 and 3 on your own.

1   **Guest**   Excuse me, the TV remote control seems to be broken.

    You   I am so sorry to hear that (A1). I will send maintenance up to your room right away to fix the remote control (A2). I assure you that this will not happen again (A3).

2   **Guest**   Excuse me, our server was rude and slow to bring our meal.

    You   **A1** _____

            A2 _____

            A3 _____

3   **Guest**   Excuse me, there is a bad odor coming from the sink.

    You   **A1** _____

            A2 _____

             A3 _____

Build Up

Match the correct solution to each situation.

> **A** Give the customer a dessert on the house.
> **B** Deduct the price of the items on the customer's bill.
> **C** Send maintenance to the guest's room.
> **D** Have the housekeeper clean the room.
> **E** Give room service as an apology.

Situation #1

The guest complains that the sink doesn't work in the bathroom and the lights went out. In this situation, as a hotel manager, what would you do for the guest?

_____

Situation #2

The customer says that he did not buy any dolls or T-shirts in your store, but they were included in the receipt. In this situation, as a store manager what is the best action you would take?

_____

Situation #3

The guest calls the front desk and says that the room is a mess and that he cannot stay in the room any longer. In this situation, as a front desk agent what would you do for the guest?

_____

Situation #4

The customer complains that the server was rude and brought out a meal that the customer did not order. In this situation, as a restaurant manager, what would you do for the customer?

_____

Situation #5

The guest says that the room is much smaller than he expected and the view of the room is terrible. In this situation, as a hotel manager, what is the best action you would take?

_____

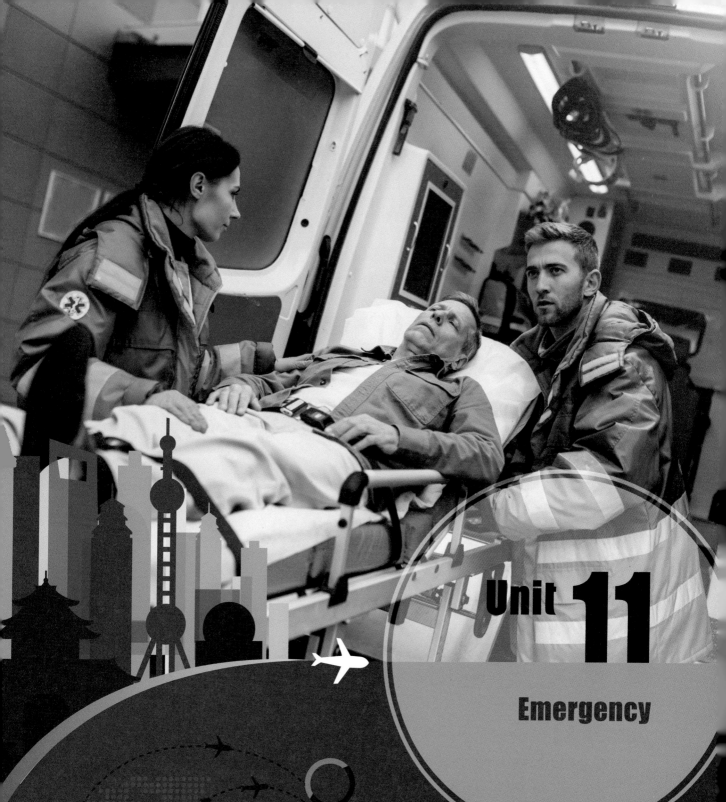

Unit **11**

Emergency

Unit 11 Emergency

Tourism English Conversation

Need-to-know Vocabulary 1

Match the words with the correct picture.

- emergency room
- injury
- medicine
- pharmacy
- indigestion
- ambulance

1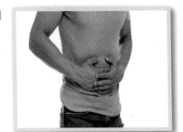

_____

2

_____

3

_____

4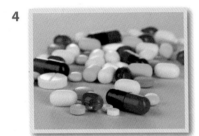

_____

5

_____

6

_____

Let's Talk 1

Practice reading the conversation with a partner and answer the questions under Check Up 1.

Tourist	Excuse me, how can I get to the pharmacy? I need to buy some medicine.
Tour Guide	I will take you there. Are you feeling sick? If you have an injury we should call the ambulance and go to the emergency room.
Tourist	That is not necessary. I am not injured.

Tour Guide	What seems to be the problem?
Tourist	It must have been something I ate, because I have indigestion.
Tour Guide	Oh no! Let's get you to the pharmacy right away and buy some medicine.
Tourist	Thank you for your help.
Tour Guide	It is not a problem. Come with me!

Idioms using "sick"

Worried sick = To be very worried   **Sick as a dog** = To be very sick

Sick at heart = To be sad or upset

Check Up 1

Circle the correct answer

1   What might have given the tourist indigestion?

   A the medicine   **B** the tour guide   **C** the pharmacy   **D** the food

2   Where does the tour guide suggest the tourist go for an injury?

   A the pharmacy   **B** the emergency room   **C** the hotel   **D** the tour

3   What will the tourist buy at the pharmacy?

   A the emergency room   **B** an ambulance   **C** some medicine   **D** an injury

Practice Pattern 1

Answer the tour guide's questions using "I need to" and the word(s) in the (   ).

1   **Tour Guide**   Why do you need to go to the pharmacy?

   Tourist   I need to + _____ . (*medicine*)

2   **Tour Guide**   Why do you need to call the ambulance?

   Tourist   I need to + _____ . (*emergency room*)

3   **Tour Guide**   Why do you need to go to the hospital?

   Tourist   I need to + _____ . (*doctor*)

Listen Up 1

Listen to the sentences and fill in the blanks with the correct word.

1   I need to go to the _____ to buy some _____.

2   Can you call the _____ for me, please?

3   I have _____ because of the food I ate during lunch.

4   We must go to the _____ right away!

5   If you have an _____, we should call the _____.

Activity 1

When would you go to the pharmacy? When would you go to the emergency room? Write down the words under the right category.

• stomach ache	• cut finger	• car accident	• headache
• twisted ankle	• food poison	• broken arm	• indigestion
• cold	• toothache	• dizziness	• sore throat
• fever	• vitamin	• pink eye	• skinned elbow

PHARMACY

EMERGENCY ROOM

Need-to-know Vocabulary 2

Fill in the blanks with the correct word and read the finished sentences out loud.

• lost and found	• embassy	• robbed	• missing
• police station	• stolen	• thief	

1   My wallet and passport were _____ when I was at the park.

2   Look in the _____ to find items you may have lost.

3   Go to the _____ to get a new passport.

4   I think a _____ came into my room and stole my luggage!

5   Can you help me find the _____ clothes from my room?

6   I was _____ last night. It was so scary!

7   The police officer will take you to the _____ to help you find the thief.

Let's Talk 2

Practice reading the conversation with a partner and answer the questions under Check Up 2.

Tourist	Excuse me, some of my belongings seem to be stolen.
Front Desk Agent	I'm sorry to hear that. Have you checked the lost and found?
Tourist	I did, but I did not find anything. I think a thief came into my room and stole my things.
Front Desk Agent	I will contact the police station immediately.
Tourist	Could you also tell me the phone number to the embassy? My passport is missing as well.
Front Desk Agent	Of course. I will get the phone number for you right away. To avoid being robbed, you should not stay out too late.
Tourist	Thank you for your advice.
Front Desk Agent	You're welcome. I'll be right back with the necessary information.

Use the following words to express that you are in a hurry (to act fast).
Immediately / Right away / As soon as possible / At once

Check Up 2

Circle T for True, or F for False.

1 The tourist has already checked the lost and found for the missing items. **T / F**

2 The tourist is missing his passport. **T / F**

3 The front desk agent suggests not to stay out too late. **T / F**

Practice Pattern 2

Put the following sentences in the correct order to make a complete dialogue between the tourist and the front desk agent.

> **A** I'm sorry to hear that. Have you checked the lost and found?
>
> **B** Could you also tell me the phone number to the embassy?
>
> **C** I will contact the police station immediately.
>
> **D** I did, but I did not find anything.
>
> **E** Of course! I will get the phone number right away.
>
> **F** Excuse me, some of my belongings seem to be missing.

Tourist _____

Front Desk Agent _____

Tourist _____

Front Desk Agent _____

Tourist _____

Front Desk Agent _____

Listen Up 2

Listen to the sentences and fill in the blanks with the correct word.

1 Could you tell me the phone number to the _____ please?

2 I will contact the _____ immediately.

3 To avoid being _____ you should not stay out too late.

4 Some of my belongings seem to be _____.

5 Have you checked the _____ for the missing items?

Activity 2

Imagine that you are a hotel employee. Try to help the guest find the missing item.

1  2  3  4

5  6  7  8

Situation #1

Guest	Hello, can you help me, please?
Hotel Employee	Sure, what can I do for you, ma'am?
Guest	I've lost something in the lobby.
Hotel Employee	These are some missing items from the lobby.
Guest	No, my item has _____.
Hotel Employee	Then, it must be this _____. Here you are, ma'am.
Guest	Oh, thank you so much!

⋯▸ **The missing item:** _____

Situation #2

Guest	Hello, please help me to find my missing item.
Hotel Employee	OK, I will, sir. Where did you lose it?
Guest	I might have lost it in the elevator.
Hotel Employee	Is that yours, the necklace case with the heart-shape?
Guest	No, my item is _____.
Hotel Employee	Then, it must be this _____. Here you are, sir.
Guest	Oh, thank you so much!

⋯▸ **The missing item:** _____

Build Up

You should always be prepared to deal with unexpected problems during a trip. Write down potential problems that could occur and the best solution.

1   What is the tourist's problem?

_____

Your solution:

_____

_____

2   What is the tourist's problem?

_____

Your solution:

_____

_____

Unit 12

Check-out

Unit 12 Check-out

Tourism English Conversation

Need-to-know **Vocabulary 1**

Use the underlined hints in the sentences to find the correct definition.

• vacate	• signature	• account
• settle	• overslept	

1   I will need your _____ on the bottom of the form.

2   Oh no, we _____! We will be late to check-out.

3   Would you take a look at your _____ to see if everything is in order?

4   You could _____ your account by cash or with a credit card.

5   What time should we _____ of our room?

Let's **Talk 1**

Practice reading the conversation with a partner and answer the questions
under **Check Up 1**.

Guest	Excuse me, we overslept! Will there be a problem with checking-out?
Front Desk Agent	Don't worry about it. You just need to vacate the room by noon and you will be alright.
Guest	Okay. I will be at the front desk by then.
Front Desk Agent	Great! You can settle your account when you come down.
Guest	Do you mind if I settle my account by cash?
Front Desk Agent	No, not at all. You can also settle your account with a credit card. We will need your signature when you settle your account.
Guest	Thank you. I will be down soon.
Front Desk Agent	See you soon.

Morning	Afternoon	Evening	Night
5AM~12PM	12PM~6PM	6MP~10PM	10PM +
Good morning	Good afternoon	Good evening	Good night

Check Up 1

Circle T for True, or F for False.

1 The guest must vacate the room by 12:00 p.m. **T / F**

2 The guest can only settle the account with a credit card. **T / F**

3 The front desk agent will need the guest's signature when settling the account. **T / F**

Practice Pattern 1

Answer the Guest's "Do you mind…" questions by filling in the blanks with the best choice from the box.

> **A** No, not at all. You can also settle your account with a credit card.
> **B** I'm afraid you will need to vacate the room by noon.
> **C** No, not at all. See you then.

1 **Guest** Do you mind if I vacate the room by 1:00 p.m.?

   Front Desk Agent _____

2 **Guest** Do you mind if I settle the account by cash?

   Front Desk Agent _____

3 **Guest** Do you mind if I go to the front desk by 12:00 p.m.?

   Front Desk Agent _____

Listen Up 1

Listen to the dialogue and circle T for True, or F for False.

1 The check-in time is at noon. **T / F**

2 The guest can settle the account from the guest room. **T / F**

3 The guest can settle the account with both cash and with a credit card. **T / F**

Activity 1

Practice using "Would (do) you mind…" **in the following activity.**

Would you mind…?
Do you mind…?

These are formal and polite ways of asking someone permission for something. However, the tricky part is how to reply to the question.

When someone asks you, **"Would you mind…?"** or **"Do you mind…?"**
If you answer "**No**," this means you are giving someone permission.
If you answer "**Yes**," this means you are NOT giving someone permission.

Therefore, No = It's OK!
            Yes = It's NOT OK!

For example,
John: Do you mind if I sit here?
Jane: Yes, I do mind.

Here, by saying "Yes," Jane does not want John to sit there.
If Jane said, "No," then Jane would be saying it was okay for John to sit there.

1

Guest	Do you mind if I settle my account with cash?
Front Desk Agent	No, not at all.

Question   Is the front desk agent saying that it is okay?

Answer   _____

Explain you answer _____

2

John	Would you mind if I borrow a dollar?
Jane	Yes, I do not have any money right now.

Question   Will Jane give a dollar to John?

Answer   _____

Explain you answer _____

Need-to-know Vocabulary 2

Fill in the blanks with the correct word and read the finished sentences out loud.

• overall	• survey	• doorman
• shuttle bus	• experience	• approximately

1 _____, the quality of service was excellent. Thank you.

2 We will be leaving in _____ 10 minutes. Please be ready to leave.

3 You can take the _____ to the airport.

4 The _____ will help you catch a taxi if you are in a hurry.

5 Could you fill out this _____ and tell us about our service?

6 We hope you had a good _____ with us.

Let's Talk 2

Practice reading the conversation with a partner and answer the questions under **Check Up 2**.

🎧 12-03

Front Desk Agent	Thank you for staying with us. Do you mind filling out this survey to tell us about our service?
Guest	Sure, the overall quality of the service was excellent. I was very pleased.
Front Desk Agent	We are so glad that you had a good experience with us.
Guest	Could you ask the doorman to catch a taxi for me? I am in a hurry.
Front Desk Agent	Of course. Where do you want to go?
Guest	I want to go to the airport.
Front Desk Agent	Then, I recommend taking the shuttle bus to the airport. It will be cheaper and it leaves in approximately 10 minutes.
Guest	That sounds better. Thank you for your help.

Approximately(= Approx.) = near, nearly exact
"uh-prok-suh=mit-ly"

Check Up 2

Circle the correct answer.

1 How does the guest feel about the hotel service?

   A It was horrible.   **B** It was terrible.   **C** It was OK.   **D** It was excellent.

2 What does the guest want the doorman to do for him?

   A to catch a fish   **B** to catch a ball   **C** to catch a taxi   **D** to catch a fly

3 What does the front desk agent recommend the guest to take to the airport?

   A a taxi   **B** an airplane   **C** the shuttle bus   **D** the shuttle plane

Practice Pattern 2

Unscramble the front desk agent's question or the guest's answer and rewrite them in the provided space.

1 **Front Desk Agent**   Could you fill out this survey to tell us about our service?

   Guest   (*the / was / Sure, / excellent / quality / overall / of / service / the*)

   _____ .

2 **Guest**   (*ask / doorman /Could / to / taxi / me / a / you / the / catch / for*)

   _____ ?

   Front Desk Agent   Of course! Where do you want to go?

3 **Guest**   I want to go to the airport.

   Front Desk Agent   (*recommend / shuttle / bus / the / taking / I / the / to / airport*)

   _____ .

Listen Up 2

Listen to the sentences and fill in the blanks with the correct word.

 12-04

1 Do you mind filling out this _____ to tell us about our service?

2 We are so glad that you had a good _____ with us.

3 Could you ask the _____ to catch a taxi for me?

4 I recommend taking the _____ to the airport.

5 It will be cheaper and it leaves in _____ 10 minutes.

Activity 2

When you work at a hotel, you should use a variety of expressions when speaking to guests for when they check out. Unscramble the expressions that you could use.

1
staying / Thank / for / us / with / you

_____

_____ .

2
you / happy / were / to / We / serve

_____

_____ .

3
will / that / you / us / again / visit /
hope / We

_____

_____ .

4
forward / look / to / seeing / again /
you / We

_____

_____ .

5
you / We / safe / home / journey / a /
wish

_____

_____ .

Build Up

Read the dialogue and fill out the survey to tell the hotel employees about their service.

Front Desk	Hello, sir. How may I help you?
Guest	I would like to check-out now. Here's my key card.
Front Desk	May I have your credit card to settle your account?
Guest	Here you are.
Front Desk	Thank you, sir. Your check-out is complete. And if you don't mind, could you give us your feedback about our overall service?
Guest	Sure. First, the check-in service was excellent. The staff members were kind and explained the hotel facilities clearly.
Front Desk	Thank you for your compliment, sir. And how did you like your room, sir?
Guest	Well… the room was a little messy but the view was great so I was satisfied.
Front Desk	We're very sorry for the messy room on your check-in day. By the way, what did you think of our valet service?
Guest	Oh, the valet service was terrible. The valet didn't even know how to park my car!
Front Desk	Oh, we're really sorry about that. We will re-train the valet and I promise that it will not happen again.
Guest	But the concierge was very nice. He was always ready to answer my questions about the popular places to visit in the city.
Front Desk	We're happy to hear that, sir. And how do you like this check-out procedure?
Guest	It's great. I think this is a very useful survey.
Front Desk	Thank you, sir. And is there anything you would like to tell us so that we could improve our service for your next visit?
Guest	Sure, I think the breakfast hours are too short. I think it could be longer.
Front Desk	OK, sir. We really appreciate you taking the time to help us. Thank you.

Thank you for your time!

– Lifetree Hotel –

1	How would you rate our check-in service?	**A** Excellent **B** Satisfactory **C** Terrible
2	How would you rate your room condition?	**A** Excellent **B** Satisfactory **C** Terrible
3	How would you rate the valet service?	**A** Excellent **B** Satisfactory **C** Terrible
4	How would you rate our concierge service?	**A** Excellent **B** Satisfactory **C** Terrible
5	How would you rate your check-out service?	**A** Excellent **B** Satisfactory **C** Terrible
6	Please leave any further comments so that we may better serve you on your next visit.	

Answer Key

Unit 01 Reservations before the Flight

Need-to-know Vocabulary 1

1 available
2 depart
3 round trip
4 class
5 reserve
6 Airlines

Check Up 1

1 T   2 F   3 T

Practice Pattern 1

1 I would like to reserve tickets to go to New York City.
2 I would like to depart on January 28th.
3 I would like to fly first class.

Listen Up 1

1 Airlines
2 round trip
3 economy
4 depart, return
5 available

Activity 1

1 January 28th
2 February 5th
3 I was born in January.
4 My favorite day of the week is Saturday.
5 Today's date is March 1st 2022.

Need-to-know Vocabulary 2

1 reservation
2 aisle
3 Visa Card
4 cancel
5 leave

6 acceptable
7 passenger

Check Up 2

1 D   2 B   3 A, C

Practice Pattern 2

1 **Airline Staff** Do you prefer a window seat or an aisle seat?
2 **Airline Staff** Ok. Your flight will leave at 10 a.m. and how will you be paying?
3 **Airline Staff** Will you be flying alone, Mr. King?

Listen Up 2

1 pay by
2 reservation
3 leave, arrive
4 alone
5 acceptable

Activity 2

credit card
alone
first class ticket
New York
February 5th

Build Up

Name: Jenny Moon   Ms
Depart: March 3rd 10 A.M.   Return: May 15th
From: New York City   To: Tokyo
Type: Round Trip
Seat: Window Seat
Class: Economy Class
Payment: Visa Card or Mastercard

Unit 02 Airport Check-in

Need-to-know Vocabulary 1

1 departure time
2 boarding gate
3 extra charge
4 scale
5 boarding pass
6 baggage claim tag
7 passport
8 baggage

Check Up 1

1 A, D   2 C   3 B

Practice Pattern 1

1 C   2 B   3 C

Listen Up 1

1 passport
2 scale
3 extra charge
4 baggage claim tags
5 departure time

Activity 1

Airline Agent	May I see your passport and boarding pass, please?
Passenger	Here is my passport and boarding pass.
Airline Agent	Where are you flying to, today?
Passenger	I am flying to Atlanta, Georgia.
Airline Agent	Do you have any baggage to check-in?
Passenger	have 1 bag to check-in.

Need-to-know Vocabulary 2

1 prohibited
2 cooperation
3 laptop
4 scanner
5 conveyor belt
6 belongings

Check Up 2

1 T   2 F   3 T

Practice Pattern 2

1 Security Check   Would you take out your laptop and put it on the conveyor belt?
2 Security Check   Would you give me any prohibited items?
3 Security Check   Would you step through the scanner?

Listen Up 2

1 belongings
2 conveyor belt
3 machine
4 cooperation
5 prohibited

Activity 2

Good afternoon passengers. This is the pre-boarding announcement for Korean Air flight 128 to New York City. We are now inviting those passengers with small children and any passengers requiring special assistance, to begin boarding at this time. Please have your boarding pass and identification ready. Regular boarding will be in approximately ten minutes. Thank you.

Build Up

For check-in   1 wine
2 perfume
3 soap
4 batteries

For boarding 1 magazine
2 MP3 Player
3 passport and boarding pass
4 smartphone

Unit 03 In the Airplane

Need-to-know Vocabulary 1

1 fasten
2 upright
3 take off
4 stow
5 seat belt
6 overhead bin

Check Up 1

1 B   2 C   3 A

Practice Pattern 1

1 **Passenger** Could you tell me the departure time?
2 **Passenger** Could you help me stow away this suitcase?
3 **Passenger** Could you help me fasten my seat belt?

Listen Up 1

1 A   2 C   3 C

Activity 1

Flight Attendant

Ladies and gentlemen, the Captain has turned on the seat belt sign. If you have not already done so, please stow your luggage underneath the seat in front of you or in an overhead bin. Please take your seat and fasten your seat belt. And also make sure your seats are in their upright positions. Thank you very much.

Need-to-know Vocabulary 2

1 monitor
2 headset
3 electronic devices
4 beverages
5 tray table
6 call button

Check Up 2

1 T   2 F   3 F

Practice Pattern 2

1 C   2 B   3 A

Listen Up 2

1 tray table
2 beverages
3 headsets
4 electronics
5 call button

Activity 2

The passenger asks for a headset, a Coke, and a blanket.

Build Up

1 Yes
2 Yes
3 No
4 No
5 Yes
6 No

Unit 04 Hotel Check-In

Need-to-know Vocabulary 1

1 key card
2 departure date

3 bellman

4 non-smoking

5 registration card

6 signature

Check Up 1

1 D   2 C   3 C

Practice Pattern 1

1 A   2 D   3 C

Listen Up 1

1 signature, card

2 departure date

3 key card

4 porter

5 non-smoking

Activity 1

1 Single room

2 Double room

3 Twin room

4 Triple room

5 Family room

6 Suite room

Need-to-know Vocabulary 2

1 lobby

2 wake-up call

3 doorman

4 receptionist

5 concierge

Check Up 2

1 A   2 C   3 B

Practice Pattern 2

1 **Answer**   The receptionist will give him a wake-up call.

2 **Answer**   The doorman will call him a taxi.

3 **Answer**   The concierge will make a dinner reservation.

Listen Up 2

1 B   2 C   3 D

Activity 2

Receptionist	Hello, how are you today?
Guest	Hi, I'm doing well. Thank you for asking.
Receptionist	How may I help you today?
Guest	I would like to check-in, please.
Receptionist	May I have your name and confirmation number?
Guest	My name is Noah Park and my confirmation number is IP090519.
Receptionist	I see your reservation Mr. Park. Do you require any special services?
Guest	Can you give me a wake-up call at 7 a.m?
Receptionist	Of course, here is your key card. Enjoy your stay.
Guest	Thank you very much.

Build Up

Reservation	Room Type	Departure Date
☑ Yes	☑ Single Room	☐ Dec. 4th
☐ No	☐ Double Room	☐ Dec. 7th
	☐ Family Room	☑ Dec. 8th
	☐ Suite	☐ Dec. 21st

Smoking	Special Request
☐ Smoking	☑ Wake-up Call
☑ Non-smoking	at 7:00
	☐ Breakfast
	☐ Laundry

Unit 05 Facilities and Amenities

Need-to-know Vocabulary 1

1 mini bar
2 continental breakfast
3 room service
4 valuables
5 complimentary
6 safe

Check Up 1

1 F   2 T   3 T

Practice Pattern 1

1 **Front Desk Agent**

You can <u>order room service to your room.</u>

2 **Front Desk Agent**

You can <u>eat breakfast in the lobby.</u>

3 **Front Desk Agent**

You can <u>put your valuables in the safe.</u>

Listen Up 1

1 Complimentary
2 room service
3 lobby
4 valuables
5 safe
6 mini bar

Activity 1

LOBBY (Breakfast)	MINI BAR	SAFE
orange juice	candy	necklace
muffin	whiskey	earrings
apple	Coca-Cola	watch
milk	chocolate bar	wallet

Need-to-know Vocabulary 2

1 swimming pool
2 sauna
3 laundry service
4 gift shop
5 fitness center
6 spa

Check Up 2

1 C   2 A   3 B

Practice Pattern 2

1 C   2 A   3 B

Listen Up 2

1 laundry service
2 swimming pool
3 spa and sauna
4 fitness center
5 spa

Activity 2

8F	⑦ <u>Swimming Pool</u>
7F	Mr. ⑥ <u>Arthur</u>'s room 701
6F	Laundry Service
5F	Mr. King's room 501 Gets a drink from the ⑤ <u>mini bar</u>
4F	Ms. Dorothy's room 412 Puts her valuables in the ④ <u>safe</u>
3F	Sauna ③ <u>Fitness Center</u>
2F	② <u>Gift Shop</u>
1F	Concierge Desk Dining Room Today's Menu: ① <u>Continental breakfast</u>

Build Up

Guest   Where can I go to swim?

You   <u>You can swim in our swimming pool.</u>

Guest   Where can I eat breakfast?

You   <u>You can eat breakfast in the lobby.</u>

Guest   Where can I get a snack?

You   <u>You can get a snack in the mini bar.</u>

Guest	Where can I put my valuables?
You	<u>You can put your valuables in the safe.</u>
Guest	Where can I buy gifts?
You	<u>You can buy gifts at the gift shop.</u>
Guest	Where can I take a steam bath?
You	<u>You can take a steam bath at the sauna.</u>

Unit 06 At a Restaurant

Need-to-know Vocabulary 1

1 server
2 appetizer
3 vegetarian
4 main entrée
5 dessert
6 menu
7 recommendation
8 specialty

Check Up 1

1 C   2 B   3 A

Practice Pattern 1

1 Customer   May I <u>have a glass of water</u>?
2 Customer   May I <u>have a salad</u>?
3 Customer   May I <u>have the Surf and Turf</u>?

Listen Up 1

1 C   2 B   3 A

Activity 1

1 Customer1   I would like my steak, <u>rare</u>.
2 Customer2   I would like my steak, <u>medium rare</u>.
3 Customer3   I would like my steak, <u>medium</u>.
4 Customer4   I would like my steak, <u>medium well</u>.
5 Customer5   I would like my steak, <u>well done</u>.

Need-to-know Vocabulary 2

1 bartender
2 liquor
3 beer
4 neat
5 on the rocks
6 cocktail
7 draft
8 wine

Check Up 2

1 T   2 F   3 F

Practice Pattern 2

1 C   2 B   3 A

Listen Up 2

1 server
2 liquors
3 wine
4 cocktail
5 neat

Activity 2

BEER	WINE	LIQUOR
Budweiser	Merlot	Scotch
Guinness	Chardonnay	Whiskey
Heineken		Rum

Build Up

Restaurant Order Form		
Appetizer	Main Entrée	Steak
□ Soup	□ Pasta	□ Rare
□ Salad	□ Pizza	□ Medium rare
□ Muesli	□ Steak	□ Medium
		□ Medium well
		□ Well done

Drink	Dessert
□ Cocktail	□ Muffin
□ Heineken	□ Cheesecake
□ Budweiser	□ Ice cream
□ Cognac	□ Coffee
□ Guinness	□ Pudding

City Information

Need-to-know Vocabulary 1

1 overcast	2 tour guide
3 entrance fee	4 museum
5 photographs	6 sunny
7 theater	8 attractions

Check Up 1

1 A   2 C   3 C

Practice Pattern 1

1 Tour Guide   You will be able to visit the museum and the theater.

2 Tour Guide   You will be able to take photographs.

3 Tour Guide   You will be able to watch a film.

Listen Up 1

1 D   2 A   3 D

Activity 1

1 Art Museum

2 Visit the shopping center, beach volleyball, explore on their own

3 Noah's Pizza

4 38 Downtown

5 9 p.m.

Need-to-know Vocabulary 2

1 crosswalk

2 intersection

3 pedestrian

4 sidewalk

5 traffic light

6 bike route

Check Up 2

1 T   2 F   3 F

Practice Pattern 2

E — B — F — C — D — A

Tourist	Excuse me, can you tell me how to get to the hotel?
Tour Guide	Sure, start at the traffic light and go straight until you reach the intersection.
Tourist	I keep going until I reach the intersection?
Tour Guide	Yes, at the intersection, you will need to turn left and you will see the hotel on the left side.
Tourist	OK. Thank you for your help.
Tour Guide	You're welcome.

Listen Up 2

Tourist	Excuse me, can you tell me how to get to the hotel?
Tour Guide	Sure, start at the traffic light and go straight until you reach the intersection. At the intersection you will need to turn left and you will see the hotel on the left side.
Tourist	Thank you for your help.

Activity 2

1 Continue towards the school. Turn left at the traffic light and follow the road. Pass the market and make the first right. The hospital will be on your left.

2 Follow the street past the Ferris wheel. Make a left turn when you see the school and turn right at the first traffic light. Go straight past the market and make the first right. The hospital will be on your left.

3 Go straight heading east and follow the road until you see the school. Turn left and go straight until you reach the first traffic light. Turn right and go straight, past the

market. Make a right turn when you see the train tracks. The hospital will be on your left.

Build Up

1 $85   2 $80

Unit 08 Transportation

Need-to-know Vocabulary 1

1 subway station
2 destination
3 heavy traffic
4 bus stop
5 taxi stand

Check Up 1

1 C   2 B   3 A

Practice Pattern 1

1	Tourist	I was wondering if <u>you could tell me what to take to get to the park.</u>
2	Tourist	I was wondering if <u>you could tell me where to take the bus.</u>
3	Tourist	I was wondering if <u>you could tell me where to take a taxi.</u>

Listen Up 1

1 subway station
2 taxi stand
3 heavy traffic
4 destination
5 bus stop

Activity 1

| 1 | subway | I always take the subway to get to work. |
| 2 | taxi stand | I am waiting for a taxi at the |

taxi stand.

3	destination	My destination is Seoul, Korea.
4	heavy traffic	There are so many cars during heavy traffic.
5	bus stop	I will wait with you at the bus stop.
6	directions	I need directions to get to the school.

Need-to-know Vocabulary 2

1 express
2 platform
3 ticket machine
4 fare
5 transfer

Check Up 2

1 C   2 C   3 B

Practice Pattern 2

1	Tourist	Can you tell me how to get there?
2	Tourist	How much is the subway fare?
3	Tourist	Do I need to transfer at all?

Listen Up 2

1 express train
2 transfer
3 ticket machine
4 platform
5 fare

Activity 2

| 1 | You | You can take the <u>green line</u> to Sadang Station. Transfer to the line number <u>4</u> and get off at Myeongdong Station. |
| 2 | You | At Shinchon Station you can take the <u>green</u> line to <u>Sindorim</u> Station. Get off there and transfer to the <u>blue</u> line heading for |

Seoul Station and get off at Yeongdeungpo Station.

3 You   Take this line towards Chungjeongno Station and get off <u>there</u>. Transfer to the <u>green</u> line towards Euljiro 3ga. City Hall Station is only one stop away.

Build Up

1 Your Explanation

Go straight on Abbey Street and turn left at the next corner. You will see a subway station when you turn. Take Line 3 to Palace Station and go 7 stops. Buckingham Palace is on Queen's Street. It will take about 30 minutes.

2 Your Explanation

Go straight until you see the crosswalk. There is a bus stop next to the crosswalk. Take bus number 1 towards Queen's Street. Get off at Palace Station and Buckingham Palace will be on the right of the station.

Unit 09 Shopping

Need-to-know Vocabulary 1

1 exchange rate
2 price
3 duty free
4 currency
5 souvenir
6 sale

Check Up 1

1 F   2 T   3 F

Practice Pattern 1

1 Tourist   How much is <u>this box of chocolates</u>?
2 Tourist   How much is <u>this T-shirt</u>?
3 Tourist   How much is <u>this perfume</u>?

Listen Up 1

1 souvenir
2 price, sale
3 gifts, duty free
4 currency
5 exchange rate

Activity 1

4. $24.31	5. $54.06	6. $103.23
A. 1 $20.00 bill	A. 1 $.50.00 bill	A. 1 $100 bill
B. 4 $1.00 bills	B. 4 $1.00 bills	B. 3 $1.00 bill
C. 1 Quarter	C. 1 Nickel	C. 2 Dimes
D. 1 Nickel	D. 1 Penny	D. 3 Pennies
E. 1 Penny		

Need-to-know Vocabulary 2

1 exchange
2 fitting room
3 refund
4 cheap
5 receipt
6 expensive

Check Up 2

1 C   2 B   3 A

Practice Pattern 2

C — F — A — D — B — E

Tourist   Excuse me, do you have a shirt that is less expensive?

Salesperson   If you look at the shirts that are on sale, you will find a shirt for a cheap price. The fitting rooms are over there if you would like to try on the clothes.

Tourist	I will not need to use a fitting room. I would like to buy this shirt now.
Salesperson	Sure, the total price is $10.00. You should keep the receipt if you want to exchange shirts or return it for a refund.
Tourist	Thank you, I will not lose the receipt.
Salesperson	You're welcome. Have a nice day!

Listen Up 2

Tourist	Excuse me, do you have a shirt less <u>expensive</u>?
Salesperson	If you look at the shirts that are on sale, you will find a shirt for a <u>cheaper</u> price. The <u>fitting rooms</u> are over there if you would like to try on the clothes.
Tourist	No, thank you. I will not need to use the fitting room. I would like to buy this shirt now.
Salesperson	Sure! The price is $10.00. You should keep the <u>receipt</u> if you want to <u>exchange</u> shirts or return it for a refund.

Activity 2

Tourist	Hello, what currency do you accept at this store?
Salesperson	Hi, we accept all currency from the dollar, won, yen, etc.
Tourist	What is the exchange rate for the Euro to Won?
Salesperson	The exchange rate for 1 Euro is 1,400 Won.
Tourist	Thank you. How much is this T-shirt?
Salesperson	This T-shirt is 30 Euros.
Tourist	Do you accept Mastercard as payment?

Salesperson	Of course!

Build Up

1	You	Your total is $23 dollars.
2	You	Your total is $40 dollars.
3	You	Your total is $7.50 dollars.

Unit 10 Complaints

Need-to-know Vocabulary 1

1 odor
2 apologize
3 inconvenience
4 assure
5 maintenance
6 defective
7 mess
8 noisy

Check Up 1

1 F	2 F	3 T

Practice Pattern 1

1	Guest	Is it possible to <u>send someone to clean my room</u>?
2	Guest	Is it possible to <u>send someone to get rid of this odor</u>?
3	Guest	Is it possible to <u>send someone to fix the TV remote control</u>?

Listen Up 1

1 mess, odor
2 maintenance
3 noisy
4 defective
5 assure

Activity 1

1 odor　　　　　　2 inconvenience
3 defective　　　　4 noisy
5 mess　　　　　　6 assure
7 maintenance　　 8 apologize

Need-to-know Vocabulary 2

1 gift certificate　 2 unsatisfied
3 replace　　　　　4 on the house
5 mistake　　　　　6 deduct

Check Up 2

1 B　　　　　　2 C　　　　　　3 B

Practice Pattern 2

1 Customer　 The server made a mistake with my meal.
2 Manager　 May I offer you a dessert on the house?
3 Manager　 I assure you that this will not happen again.

Listen Up 2

1 D　　　　　　2 D　　　　　　3 B

Activity 2

1 A1　I am so sorry to hear that.
　A2　I will send maintenance up to your room right away to fix the remote control.
　A3　I assure you that this will not happen again.
2 A I　I apologize about that.
　A2　May I offer you a dessert on the house as compensation?
　A3　Once again, I am truly sorry about that and I assure you that this will not happen again.
3 A1　I am sorry to hear that.
　A2　I will send someone up to your room right away to fix this issue.

A3　Once again, I am truly sorry about the inconvenience. I assure you this problem will be fixed immediately.

Build Up

1 C　Send maintenance to the guest's room.
2 B　Deduct the price of the items on the customer's bill.
3 D　Have the housekeeper clean the room.
4 A　Give the customer a dessert on the house.
5 E　Give room service as an apology.

Unit 11 Emergency

Need-to-know Vocabulary 1

1 indigestion
2 ambulance
3 emergency room
4 medicine
5 injury
6 pharmacy

Check Up 1

1 D　　　　　　2 B　　　　　　3 C

Practice Pattern 1

1 Tourist　 I need to buy some medicine.
2 Tourist　 I need to go to the emergency room.
3 Tourist　 I need to see the doctor.

Listen Up 1

1 pharmacy, medicine
2 ambulance
3 indigestion
4 emergency room
5 injury, ambulance

Activity 1

PHARMACY	EMERGENCY ROOM
stomach ache	car accident
cut finger	twisted ankle
headache	food poison
indigestion	broken arm
cold	dizziness
toothache	fever
sore throat	skinned elbow
vitamin	
pink eye	

Need-to-know Vocabulary 2

1 stolen

2 lost and found

3 embassy

4 thief

5 missing

6 robbed

7 police station

Check Up 2

1 T   2 T   3 T

Practice Pattern 2

F — A — D — C — B — E

Tourist	Excuse me, some of my belongings seem to be missing.
Front Desk Agent	I'm sorry to hear that. Have you checked the lost and found?
Tourist	I did, but I did not find anything.
Front Desk Agent	I will contact the police station immediately.
Tourist	Could you also tell me the phone number to the embassy?
Front Desk Agent	Of course! I will get the phone number right away.

Listen Up 2

1 embassy   2 police station

3 robbed   4 missing

5 lost and found

Activity 2

Situation 1

Guest	Hello, can you help me, please?
Hotel Employee	Sure, what can I do for you, ma'am?
Guest	I've lost something in the lobby.
Hotel Employee	These are some missing items from the lobby.
Guest	No, my item has a strap and can tell the time.
Hotel Employee	Then, it must be this watch. Here you are, ma'am.
Guest	Oh, thank you so much!

⋯▸ **The missing item** Watch

Situation 2

Guest	Hello, please help me to find my missing item!
Hotel Employee	OK, I will, sir. Where did you lose it?
Guest	I might have lost it in the elevator.
Hotel Employee	Is that yours, the necklace case with the heart-shape?
Guest	No, my item is long and wraps around my waist.
Hotel Employee	Then, it must be this belt. Here you are, sir.
Guest	Oh, thank you so much!

⋯▸ **The missing item** Belt

1 What is the tourist's problem?

The tourist has a leg injury.

Your solution

Call an ambulance so you can go to the emergency room.

2 What is the tourist's problem?

The tourist has lost some items from the room.

Your solution

Look for the items in the lost and found.

Unit 12 Check-out

Need-to-know Vocabulary 1

1 signature 2 overslept 3 account

4 settle 5 vacate

Check Up 1

1 T 2 F 3 T

Practice Pattern 1

1 B 2 A 3 C

Listen Up 1

1 F 2 F 3 T

Activity 1

1 Question	Is the front desk agent saying that it is okay?
Explain your answer	Yes, it is okay. "No" here is giving permission to a request.
2 Question	Will Jane give a dollar to John?
Explain your answer	No, because "Yes" here is denying a request.

Need-to-know Vocabulary 2

1 Overall 2 approximately

3 shuttle bus 4 doorman

5 survey 6 experience

Check Up 2

1 D 2 C 3 C

Practice Pattern 2

1 Guest Sure, the overall quality of the service was excellent.

2 Guest Could you ask the doorman to catch a taxi for me?

3 Guest I recommend taking the shuttle bus to the airport.

Listen Up 2

1 survey 2 experience

3 doorman/valet 4 shuttle bus

5 approximately

Activity 2

1 Thank you for staying with us.

2 We were happy to serve you.

3 We hope that you will visit us again.

4 We look forward to seeing you again.

5 We wish you a safe journey home.

Build Up

1 A 2 B 3 C

4 A 5 A

6 Perhaps you can extend the breakfast hours.